EXARCH
LEONID FEODOROV

BRIDGEBUILDER BETWEEN
ROME AND MOSCOW

Exarch
Leonid Feodorov

BRIDGEBUILDER BETWEEN
ROME AND MOSCOW

By Paul Mailleux, S.J.

P. J. KENEDY & SONS
NEW YORK

Imprimi potest: John J. McGinty, S.J.
Praep. Prov. Neo-Ebor.
New York, February 29, 1964

Nihil obstat: Daniel V. Flynn, J.C.D.
Censor Librorum
Imprimatur: ✠ Francis Cardinal Spellman
Archbishop of New York
March 5, 1964

Copyright © 1964 by P.J. Kenedy & Sons
All Rights Reserved
L.C. Card: 64-14560
Printed in the United States of America

Contents

EXARCH
LEONID FEODOROV

BRIDGEBUILDER BETWEEN
ROME AND MOSCOW

Introduction

IF specialists in international espionage read the following story—and we hope they will—they may feel a certain professional jealousy of the author's sources of information. How could a biographer collect so many details about a priest who spent the last and most tragic years of his eventful life, not only behind the most rigid iron curtain that history has ever known, but in concentration camps and forests of northern Russia where no foreigner has been allowed to travel since 1917, nor private correspondence permitted to circulate?

Surprisingly enough, collecting this information did not require any particular craftiness. A small number of foreigners were, at different periods, released from these concentration camps. These were mostly French, Poles and Latvians. There they had met Exarch Feodorov and he had made a deep impression on them. From the memories of these former prisoners it was possible to reconstruct the living conditions of the camps, and thus to follow Father Leonid step by step. One of his friends did try to reach him during the last weeks of his life—and it is through him that we have learned the circumstances of his death.

Providentially, an American Jesuit, Father Edmund A. Walsh, director of the Pontifical Mission of aid to Russia at the time of the famine of 1921–22, together with a British correspondent of the *New York Herald,* Captain Francis McCullagh, found themselves in Moscow at the time of Father Feodorov's arrest. Both conceived the highest admiration for him, followed his trial attentively, and left an accurate stenographic report of it. The dynamic American Jesuit developed a profound admiration for the Exarch. After leaving Russia, Father Walsh fulfilled other important missions: in the name of the Holy See he conducted delicate negotiations with the Mexican government; he next prepared the foundation of a Catholic school of higher education at Bagdad, and he founded the School of Foreign Service at Georgetown University. During his lifetime he met many outstanding men, yet none left so vivid an impression on him as did the Exarch. Until his death, one of the rare portraits on the walls of his room at Georgetown was that of Father Feodorov, painted by a Russian artist of Rome, Paul Maltzev.

Exarch Leonid also had admirers and devoted friends among his compatriots outside the Soviet Union. Among the most faithful and active was Prince Peter Mikhailovich Volkonsky. A few lines about him and the situation of Russian converts to Catholicism at that period will help the reader to understand how the details of Father Feodorov's life were collected.

Throughout the centuries the Russian Orthodox Church has been the national church of Russia. It was unthinkable that the Czar would not have been an Orthodox; and if anybody in Russia was, for instance, a Protestant or a Catholic, one could be sure that he was of foreign origin. Nevertheless, during the first part of the nineteenth century some distinguished members of the Russian aristocracy became Catholic. To avoid the difficulties which their change of religion would have provoked in Russia, they all went abroad and never returned to their native land.

Such was the case of Madame Sophie Swetchine who, from 1815 to 1857, lived in France and played an important role among the French intellectuals of that time.[1] Such was also the case—among others—of Prince John Gagarine who became a Jesuit, and in 1856 founded the well-known French review, *Les Etudes*, in Paris.[2] Two members of the Russian nobility became outstanding pioneers of Catholic life in the United States. Prince Dimitri Golitzine was ordained a Catholic priest in Maryland and founded the famous mission of Loretto for the isolated Irish and German settlers of Pennsylvania. His friend and admirer, Baron Maltitz, the Russian Ambassador to Washington, helped him very generously.[3] Father Dimitri died in 1840, but in that same year his distant cousin, Elizabeth Golitzine, who had been received into the Catholic Church and had become one of the first members of the congregation called the Religious of the Sacred Heart, arrived in the United States. Sent to America to visit and organize the houses of that congregation, she died in Louisiana in 1843.[4]

All these Russian Catholics living outside Russia had adopted the Roman rite, that is, the religious customs of the Catholics among whom they found themselves. Only toward the end of the century did some Russians secretly become Catholic in Russia itself, trying to remain faithful not only to their country but to its liturgical traditions as well.

The first of these was Princess Elizabeth Volkonsky, born in 1838. In her adult life this remarkable woman studied Latin and Greek in order to be able to read the Scriptures and the writings of the Church Fathers in the original. This reading led her into the Catholic Church in 1887. Later, in her estate of the Tambov Government (Province), 260 miles southeast of Moscow, she wrote in Russian two studies on the Church.[5]

In these books she gave the conclusions of her reading and studies, but they had to be printed abroad to avoid governmental censorship. She died in St. Petersburg in 1897, after receiving the last rites from the French Dominican Father Lagrange.

Her daughter Marie and three of her four sons followed her later into the Catholic Church. One of them, Prince Alexander Volkonsky, was a general in the Imperial Russian Army and later became a Catholic priest. He wrote several books on Russian history and the teaching of the Catholic Church.[6] He died in Rome in 1934. His brother Peter, in Petrograd, became the friend and spiritual son of Father Leonid Feodorov. After leaving Russia he started faithfully collecting the letters and writings of the Exarch and testimonies about him. From Paris, where he had emigrated, he made several trips to Poland and to Italy to gather these documents. Prince Peter Volkonsky died in 1945, too soon to write the book he had planned, but leaving a priceless collection of documents which have made the present biography possible.

In Russian letters Father Leonid's last name is spelled 'Fedorov,' but all through this biography we have spelled it 'Feodorov,' as he used to write it himself when he resided in Western Europe and as it should be pronounced. In Russian, when the accent of a word falls on 'e' followed by a hard consonant, that 'e' is generally pronounced as 'o.' Therefore, to be consistent, we have spelled the other Russian names, such as Soloviov, Mohiliov, as they are pronounced.

CHAPTER ONE

St. Petersburg

NINE o'clock in the morning. Every school day in the Second Gymnasium in St. Petersburg began with the same ritual: the uniformed pupils filed into the main hall where the school chaplain, an Orthodox priest with a long beard and hair down to his shoulders, the Byzantine stole hanging nearly to his feet, stood waiting for them in front of an icon of the Virgin. When they were all inside, a pupil of the senior class recited the morning prayer and read a passage from the Gospels; then, before leaving the room, each boy came and stood, with head lowered and hands placed one above the other on a level with his chest, to receive the priest's blessing. As they passed before the principal of the Gymnasium, each of them gave him a military salute, and then they went into their respective classrooms. The rest of the day was spent, as in schools throughout the world, in lessons broken by short periods of recreation.

The Gymnasium (the Russian high school) at this time brought together young men of varied social backgrounds. Every morning heavy barouches or sleighs set down at its doors the sons of the St. Petersburg aristocracy, to whom money meant as little as the air they breathed. With them, through the same doors, entered the sons of artisans or small tradesmen who wanted to rise in society, and who sometimes showed a touch of bitterness toward their more fortunate schoolfellows. The discipline of the school was military in pattern, and the efforts and attention of the masters were concentrated far more on the intellectual development of the pupils than on their moral education. The young boys of twelve had already read books of every sort, and a certain supervisor of the boarders, wishing to make himself popular, made a speciality of telling smutty stories. The boys themselves did not know how to react for they were paralyzed by their respect for the opinions of others. . . .

This is the school background in which the recollections of one of his fellow pupils give us our first picture of Leonid Feodorov. He had joined the Second Gymnasium on a September morning in 1890, and was to spend eight years there, acquiring a secondary education based on an intensive study of the classical languages.

A few lines written by his mother in a family diary tell us something of his earlier years:

"Leonid was born on November 4, 1879," she wrote, "on a Sunday, at 6 o'clock in the morning.

"Leonid made his first confession to Father Bogdanovsky at the age of seven.

"He learned to read and write at the age of six.

"When he was eight he went to school at Akkerman.

"When he was eleven he joined the Second Gymnasium in St. Petersburg, in the second section of the first class."

The last detail is significant, for in fact pupils of somewhat modest background were usually placed by the principal of the school in the second section, the first section being re-

served for the day boarders, most of whom came from rich
families.

Indeed, Leonid's family was of humble origin. His grand-
father, Theodore Sakharovich Feodorov, was a crown serf of
the Government of Yaroslav, to the north of Moscow; in 1861
Czar Alexander's liberation edict had given him his freedom,
and his son John, Leonid's father, had moved to St. Petersburg, where he opened an inexpensive restaurant in the busi-
ness quarter. This restaurant was called the *Malii Yaroslavietz*
—"The Little Yaroslavian,"—and acquired a good reputation. John died prematurely from the effects of overwork and
vicissitude, leaving his wife and Leonid, his only child. After
her husband's death Madame Feodorov continued to run the
restaurant alone, and decided to put aside the 15,000 rubles
he had left her so that she could spend them all on Leonid's
education.

Lyubov Dimitryevna Feodorov, Leonid's mother, was of
Greek origin, a woman in whom remarkable courage was
allied to great sensitivity, a special feeling for harmony and
order, and also exceptional rectitude. She remained a widow,
and kept all her affection for her son, whom she called
"Lionia"—the Russian diminutive of his name. At this time
"Lionia" was a gentle, delicate adolescent, slim, very fair-
skinned, with curly reddish hair. Among his schoolfellows his
graceful appearance had earned him the nickname "Eva,"
which remained with him until he left school.

Fifteen years later, as a Studite monk, he wrote down some
of his childhood memories. He was then going through a
period of great austerity, and his criticisms of his former
schoolfellows were very harsh. In the opinion of some of his
contemporaries they were too harsh, and we should no doubt
make allowances for this when we consider some of the more
severe of them. "Idealists of my type," he writes, "had a hard

time at the Gymnasium. There were few young men there
who longed for higher things, and they were regarded with
general disdain." And he adds: "I think that everyone liked
me for my good nature, but they could not forgive my ideal-
ism. . . ." "Our Gymnasium was a cesspool of every vice," he
continues. "Our student gatherings all ended in drunkenness,
debauchery and brutality. . . ." [1]

Meanwhile he hoped to find support in a deeper friendship
with one of his companions. This friendship lasted long after
they had left school, but it was of no help to him, for the
young man on whom he had relied let himself be carried away
in the general stream. Leonid admits that from time to time
in conversation he himself let slip what he calls "trivial and
cynical" remarks, but his personal conduct, on the other
hand, was irreproachable.

"I then fell in love," he tells us, "with a young girl who was
simple and good but shy and awkward, and not at all good
looking. The other boys made fun of her and referred to her
as 'that stupid savage.' 'What you young fools like,' I thought,
'is someone with a pretty face and a glib tongue, because your
minds are incapable of appreciating anything else. Well, I am
going to show you whom to love and how.' " And he points
out: "This incident brought into my head, I think for the first
time, the Pharisaic idea—'I am not like other men'; but I did
not add, 'I thank Thee, Lord,' because I felt that I had acquired this by my own will and my independent character."

From an early age he was an avid reader. No one directed
his choice of books and his inexperienced mother let herself
be guided in this matter by unrealistically optimistic principles. "A young man of your age should read everything," she
told her son. "The clash of ideas will bring you understanding." "So I began to devour the best-known French novelists
—Zola, Hugo, Maupassant and Dumas. I became acquainted
with the Italian Renaissance and its corrupt literature—

Boccaccio and Ariosto—and with the products of the German *Zerstreuung*. My head came to be like a sewer into which the foulest muck was emptied."

Gradually the confusion of ideas and the spectacle of corruption caused a progressive loss of spiritual energy in the young man and brought with it fear of life and hatred of the world. He had read Schopenhauer and Hartmann when some works of Hindu philosophy happened to come into his hands. "Reading them from sutra to sutra," he says, "I felt as if I was reading my own thoughts: What is the use of this worthless life? What is the use of activity, agitation, generous impulses, effort? Surely the perpetual rest of Nirvana, in which all ambition fades and in which we find the eternal peace of annihilation, is preferable to them. It is better to stay still than to go forward; it is better to sit than to stand; it is better to sleep than to keep awake; the ideal is to annihilate oneself. . . ."

This attitude of mind was, moreover, encouraged by his physical condition. The *Malii Yaroslavietz* was right in the center of St. Petersburg, and the activity of the restaurant continued late into the night, disturbing his sleep. This made him less than ever able to control his natural impressionability. However, these crises were only superficial, for deep in his soul he was unharmed, and he retained the love of order and harmony which his mother's Greek background had given her, and which she struggled to develop in him. "When I was nine," he writes, "I was already reading classical mythology and ancient history. I went progressively deeper into the heart of the ancient world, and I studied its every detail. Constantly in my childhood I dreamed of ancient Greece. In this way I developed a love of beauty which has on many occasions protected me from moral falls, but at the same time it increased my aversion for the world in which I had to live. There, in the distant past, I discovered the arts, beauty, a

purely aesthetic existence, and the soaring aspirations of
minds still young. Here, I was suffocating in the atmosphere
of factories and shops which were simply reminders of the
struggle for existence, superficiality, vulgarity, mean instincts
and cupidity. I was left with nostalgia for a paradise irrevoca-
bly lost. . . ."

For some time this wish to escape from his daily life made
him dream of a career filled with chivalrous exploits: "I could
think only of one thing," he tells us, "which was to become a
soldier—a real soldier who dedicates himself to his vocation
to the extent of entire self-forgetfulness. . . . I liked to repeat
Wordsworth's statement: 'War is the daughter of God,' and I
delighted in the *Memoirs* of Moltke. After all, is it not right
that from time to time the world should be shaken up and
raised above its low inclinations, and is not war the one thing
that interrupts our ordinary humdrum lives and inspires us
with more noble ambitions? . . . At times my vivid imagination pictured the total destruction of modern civilization and
a return of the world to primitive simplicity. . . ."

Madame Feodorov had done everything to inculcate in him
Christian piety, but, at the very moment when his mind was
beginning to develop the sensitive boy was disillusioned by
an unfortunate incident. The Orthodox Church has kept the
custom of giving the Eucharist even to young children. After
her son's baptism, Madame Feodorov had often carried him
in her arms to their parish church so that he could take holy
Communion. As is the custom in Russia, when the little boy
was seven she prepared him for making his first confession.
Lionia approached this with great seriousness, and in the
days preceding it he fasted, went to church and assiduously
sought out his least sins. Unfortunately he chanced on a
mediocre confessor who was heedless of his fervor. Instead,
recognizing him as the boy from the *Malii Yaroslavietz*, he
said: "Hello, Lionia; how are your parents? Tell them that I

will be 'round tomorrow for a meal, and that I'd like them
to prepare my favorite stew. . . ." Deeply wounded, Leonid
left with the vague feeling that he had been naive to have
taken so much trouble in this matter. He was never to forget
this incident, and forty years later, in a moment of self-revela-
tion, he confided it to a friend.

Fortunately he was to meet during his schooldays a spiritual
guide with far greater breadth of vision. When he reached the
upper classes in the Second Gymnasium he found that his
religious teacher was one of the most remarkable Russian
Orthodox priests of his time, Father Constantine Smirnov.[2]

Father Constantine was a very learned man of God who had
an exceptional influence over the young men in his charge.
Russia was then in the early stages of a period of unrest
which was to lead to the Revolution of 1905. The younger
generation, in its thirst for reform, was interested solely in
overthrowing the established order, and too often associated
religion with politics. Father Constantine, conscious of his
pastoral responsibilities, strove above all to help his young
students to understand the transcendent and wholly spiritual
mission of the Church of Christ. He suffered at seeing the
Russian Church becoming a national organism, too submis-
sive to the human aspirations of the government, and too
little free to fulfill its purely spiritual mission. The superiority
of the Church over all other societies, and the sublimity of its
role in the world, were his favorite themes when he taught or
preached. And as his goodness and learning were allied to
extraordinary ability as a teacher, he managed to awake enthusiasm for his ideals in a good number of his pupils.

It was unusual in Russia for young men from the intellectual classes to contemplate entering the priesthood. Seminarians were recruited almost exclusively from among the
sons of diocesan priests, whose families formed a sort of
priestly caste. In the Second Gymnasium at St. Petersburg,

Father Constantine, through his deep influence on his pupils, broke this tradition. During the time that he taught there, several sons of the most wealthy families of the capital decided to dedicate their lives to the service of the Church. The friendship that developed between young Leonid Feodorov and his religious teacher was to last after Leonid's years at the Gymnasium. Under the direction of this spiritual guide, Leonid's vague desire to work toward building a better world became clearer. After eight years at secondary school, he passed his final examinations with such success that he was awarded the gold medal; because of this, he also obtained the certificate of Completion of Studies officially awarded by the Ministry of Public Education.

As his spirit grew calmer his former dreams of a military career faded. On leaving the Gymnasium and finding himself obliged to choose a higher educational establishment, Leonid decided to enter the Ecclesiastical Academy.

In Czarist Russia each eparchy or diocese of the Orthodox Church had its seminary for training the priests of the diocesan clergy, who were known as the 'white' clergy. As future pastors of parishes, these priests had to marry before they were ordained deacons. In addition to these seminaries, there were in St. Petersburg, Moscow, Kiev and Kazan, four theological colleges called "Ecclesiastical Academies." To these were sent, for more advanced training, members of the 'white' clergy and of the 'black' clergy (monks), who were destined to become teachers or to fill the higher offices of the Church. Since celibacy was obligatory for the bishops, they were in fact always chosen from among the priests of the 'black' clergy.

The Ecclesiastical Academy of St. Petersburg was a section of the Alexander Nevski *lavra,* a huge monastery situated to the east of the city along the banks of the Neva. Leonid Feodorov was admitted in 1898.

It would be a mistake to conceive of the internal organization of these academies in terms of our knowledge of Catholic seminaries reformed by the Council of Trent. They were attended not only by boarding pupils who received scholarships from the state, but also by a fair number of free pupils who lived at home. Neither class of pupil wore the cassock, but a uniform which was rather military in appearance; they were allowed great freedom in their movements. Only a minority of them were ordained priests at the end of their four years of study; the others remained laymen, and generally went into the administrative services of the Church or of the Ministry of Religions. The most brilliant continued for a further two or three years, preparing a thesis in order to obtain the degree of master of divinity.

In the Academy, as in the Gymnasium, Leonid applied himself to his studies as seriously as he could. He supplemented them by reading books that were relevant to the scholastic curriculum and to his interests at the time. They were to cause in him a profound disturbance and a crisis which, this time, was to indicate the final direction of his life.

CHAPTER TWO

The Decisive Step

MADAME Feodorov's restaurant was a gourmet's paradise. It
was also one of the favorite haunts of the intellectuals of the
capital—and God knows how numerous they were in St.
Petersburg, the Russian Athens of that period! They came
to "The Little Yaroslavian" to exchange ideas and voice their
desire for reform, all the more anxious to meet because, due
to stringent governmental censorship, it was difficult for them
to express their views in writing.

It was during this last part of the nineteenth century that
the Russian intelligentsia began to react against the materialism which had appealed to a rather large number of its members during the preceding decades. The harbinger of this new
trend was Vladimir Soloviov, a young and brilliant professor
of philosophy. Son of a famous Russian historian, he was a
poet, a philosopher and a theologian who had given up a
promising academic career in order to devote his time more
freely to the dissemination of his ideas. Keenly perceptive, he
had foretold the cataclysms threatening humanity, and more
particularly those menacing Russia. He was insistent on the
responsibility of Christians in a world in which change was

rapid and hazardous. He vigorously preached return to integral Christianity, justice for the Jews, and above all Russia's reconciliation with the Holy See. When Soloviov died, on July 31, 1900, he was only forty-seven years old, but he had made a deep impression on a goodly number of his compatriots. During his last years he had divided his activities between Moscow and St. Petersburg, and, when in the capital, he often took his meals and met his friends at the *Malii Yaroslavietz*. Leonid never missed an opportunity to listen to him and ask him innumerable questions.[1]

It was Father Constantine Smirnov who had awakened young Feodorov's deep love for the Church while he was attending the gymnasium, but at that time this feeling was directed toward the Russian Orthodox Church, that outgrowth of the Byzantine Church of the East which was responsible for the Christian character peculiar to the Russian nation, and for the saving of the country during the most tragic hours of her history. Although Soloviov rekindled this devotion in young Feodorov, at the same time he invited him to look beyond some of the narrowness of the national Church and helped him to find his place in the universal Christian family by urging him to study the claims of the Roman Church with more objectivity than was customary among his compatriots in those days.

"I was already twenty years old," Leonid wrote some time later,[2] "when through the reading of the Fathers and of history, I was able to discover the true Universal Church. Divine grace touched me at the right time, that is to say, at a time when I was losing my faith. A complete reversal took place within me. The Savior, who had shed His blood for humanity, lived once again in my thoughts. I became a confirmed believer, an ardent defender of Christianity, and I decided to devote my life to the defense and expansion of the Church. . . ."

Being of a determined nature, he decided to pursue his study of Catholicism as far as possible, and to make enquiries at St. Catherine's, the main Catholic Church of St. Petersburg, which was Polish and of the Latin rite. He found the rector, Father Ivan Stislavsky, devout as well as understanding; he received Leonid, answered his questions, and suggested that he join the group of young men who met periodically at his home. At the Ecclesiastical Academy, Leonid applied himself more attentively to his theological studies than did any of his fellow students; moreover, his classmates observed his tendency to defend the positions of the Roman Church, and one of his teachers too took the habit of calling him "our Catholic" whenever he addressed him during the classes.

"My decision to become a priest," he wrote, "was irrevocable." But how to achieve this result was the problem. "In the Russian Church, the priests [diocesan] were required to marry, and I was loath even to think of such a thing. Neither did I want to join the Catholic Church immediately. What I wanted was to finish my studies at the Ecclesiastical Academy, and then, after two or three years of priesthood in the Orthodox Church, to write a thesis and become a master of divinity.* The only possible solution, therefore, was to become a monk. To tell the truth, receiving the monastic tonsure would have been a mere formality for me had I decided to take such a step. In Russia, educated monks could dispense with the novitiate and did not need to submit to the usual tests. The students of the Ecclesiastical Academy, once they were in their third year, could wear the religious habit after only a month of preparation. They were ordained deacons eight days later, and could then live anywhere unhampered by any restriction. This kind of life appealed to me. It would free me from the necessity of marrying, as well as from

* The doctorate of divinity was exceptional in Russia.

all material worries. It would enable me to integrate my whole life and concentrate exclusively on improving my spiritual life."

But Leonid rejected a way of life in which the gift of self to others would hardly have found a place, and egotism could easily have played a dominant part. "I came to understand," he wrote, "that genuine monasticism is not Buddhism, nor the 'turning inward' as implied by Palamas,* but self-improvement through an obstinate struggle against one's own unrestrained tendencies, and the following of Christ. The monk cannot live on this earth merely in search of peace. He must, on the contrary, forever lend an ear to the voice of Christ, which tells him to be perfect as the Heavenly Father is perfect, and strive with all his strength toward making this ideal come true."

We can only wonder at the struggle which took place in the depths of his soul, and which led him to take the decisive step without waiting any longer. He kept this a secret, and to guess at it would be to risk deviating from the truth. Later, in a letter in which he set down a few autobiographical notes, he wrote without further comment: "I finally resolved to take a step from which there was no turning back. I decided to leave for a foreign country in order to become a Catholic."

He did not realize what this step would cost him!

To understand the general attitude of Russia toward the Roman Catholic Church, it is well to go back to the first centuries of Christianity and to consider the development of the Church in the Western Latin countries on the one hand, and in the Greco-Byzantine Orient on the other.[3]

---

* Gregory Palamas, a fourteenth-century Byzantine monk of Mount Athos who, according to tradition, advocated an elaborate system of asceticism, detachment from earthly cares, submission to an approved superior, prayer, and perfect repose of body and will. His influence on Orthodox monasticism was profound.

Within the Roman Empire—the cradle of Christianity—the Christians were at first only a scorned and persecuted minority, and so remained for three centuries. At the beginning of the fourth century, after the conversion of the Roman Emperor Constantine, not only did they acquire the rights of citizenship, but they also rapidly began to take an active part in the life of the community. This Emperor seems at first to have wished to confine himself to the protection of the Church without interfering in its internal affairs, but the heresies which arose at that time endangered the political unity of the Empire. Consequently, he changed his attitude, intervened more often in religious matters, and summoned the Council of Nicea, which was to be the first of the Ecumenical Councils.

A few years later, in order to govern and defend the Empire more efficiently, Constantine founded a second capital at Byzantium—a New Rome. The political split of the Empire was to follow within a few years. This political division was to have the most profound ecclesiastical repercussions. In the course of the following centuries the Roman Empire of the West gradually broke up, giving rise to many independent States. Confronted with this situation, the successive Bishops of Old Rome were to affirm the Church's supranational role and define more and more fully and clearly the supreme pastoral mission with which they were invested as heirs to Peter's apostolate. Indefatigable protectors of the integrity of doctrine, they zealously guarded the independence and unity of the Church against the encroachments of the civil authorities.

In Byzantium, on the other hand, the old traditions of the Roman Empire were retained for another ten centuries, until 1453. In this old Empire, the emperor, who was also the *Pontifex Maximus*, i.e. the Supreme Pontiff, had presided over religious as well as civic life, and this undivided sovereignty the Byzantine emperor also claimed. As God's representative on earth, he sought to provide completely not only for the temporal but for the spiritual welfare of his subjects. Thus in Byzantium the need of a supranational ecclesiastical primacy was not realized as it had been in Rome. It was the difference between these two conceptions which caused the basic disagreement between the Roman Catholic Church and the Orthodox Church of the East.

Political conflicts soon arose to stiffen this opposition between East and West. The shameful brutalities of the Crusaders, and their sack of Constantinople at the beginning of the thirteenth century, kindled a tenacious and lasting animosity against the Latins in the hearts of all the Greeks. It became impossible to discuss matters in any spirit of brotherhood.

The Crusaders, their generosity and their vaunted valor notwithstanding, usually lacked the culture and finesse which would have been necessary to understand and respect the Greek religious tradition. They placed a Latin patriarch in the Cathedral of Santa Sophia in Constantinople, which had been the see of St. John Chrysostom, of Photius, and of so many other famous patriarchs of the Byzantine Church. They established a Latin hierarchy in the Christian Orient and placed it over and above the Eastern hierarchy. By so doing, they introduced a kind of Latin paternalism (Eastern Christians would probably call it "colonialism"!) which inevitably impeded mutual understanding and, as a result, friendship.

Later, after the capture of Constantinople by the Turks and the destruction of the Byzantine Empire, Moscow—the Third Rome, i.e., Russia—inherited the Byzantine influence in the Eastern Christian world, and at the same time formed its own conception of the relationship between the temporal power and the Church. Just as the Crusades had engendered intense animosity between Greek and Latin, so from the sixteenth century onward the wars between Poland and

Russia increased still more the antagonism which divided Catholics and Orthodox. To this was added the fact that through a regrettable set of circumstances the Roman Church had seemed the staunch ally of Russia's enemies, while, on the other hand, the national Orthodox Church during the course of many centuries had often saved the nation at crucial hours when the political power had faltered. Venerated because of this, it seemed to be somehow indispensable to the life of the Russian nation, and to separate from it seemed tantamount to leaving the Russian community itself.

There were Catholics in Russia, of course, but they were all of foreign origin. Throughout Russia not a single Catholic church held services in the Russian language. The mother tongue of the Catholics was Polish nearly everywhere, the majority of the faithful being Poles who had been transplanted to Russia, more often than not involuntarily, following reprisals carried out by the Russian police either against themselves or against their forebears. Consequently they remained foreigners, often opposed to Russian national ambitions, and they strengthened the impression already held by the Russians that Catholicism was a foreign importation, essentially hostile to their native land. On the other hand, the government was absolutely opposed to a genuinely *Russian Catholic Church,* that is, a Church in which the faithful could pray according to the Byzantine rite, and at the same time would recognize the Pope as the supreme pontiff of that Church.

Moreover, Russian legislation made it practically impossible at that time for any Orthodox to become a Catholic. According to the laws, his property would be confiscated, and the Catholic priest welcoming him into the fold would be deported to Siberia.[4] Emigration was necessary if one wanted to become a Catholic. A Protestant or a Jew wishing to embrace Catholicism in Russia would have had to face similar difficulties. At the end of the nineteenth century there were still privileged state religions in several countries and Orthodoxy occupied that position in Russia. It was not compulsory, of course; other religions were tolerated, but any proselytism on their part was forbidden, since this remained the monopoly of the state religion. Therefore, after long reflection and in order to abide by what he considered to be the will of Christ, young Leonid had to leave his country.

To leave Russia, he needed a passport, and to obtain this passport he had to have the authorization to interrupt his studies at the Ecclesiastical Academy. He went to see Bishop Theophanus, then the Dean of the Academy, who received him with kindness and said:

"I know very well why you want to go to Italy. . . . So be it, and may God keep you."

His mother, who had witnessed his anguish and his search for truth with affection and respect, did not try to hold him back, and even promised to help him as much as she possibly could. On June 19, 1902, Leonid embraced her lovingly and left home, accompanied by Father Stislavsky, the pastor of St. Catherine's. He was on his way to Rome.

map of RUSSIA—

SHOWING THE CITIES
MENTIONED IN THE
BIOGRAPHY

Artic Ocean

White Sea

SOLOVKI

PINEGA

ARCHANGEL

KOTLAS

TOBOLSK

Baltic Sea

PETROGRAD

VIATKA

YAROSLAV

Europe

Ural Mountains

Asia

NIZHNI NOVGOROD

MOSCOW

MOHILIOV

KALUGA

UFA

BRIANSK

LVOV

KIEV

SARATOV

KHARKOV

Siberia

LUGANSK

ODESSA

Black Sea

Caucasus

Caspian Sea

CONSTANTINOPLE

CHAPTER THREE

Seminarian in Italy

THE direct road from St. Petersburg to Rome passes through Warsaw and Vienna. At the beginning of their journey, Father Stislavsky and his young companion went slightly out of their way to stop at Lvov. The city, called Lvov by the Russians, Lviv by the Ukrainians, and Lemberg by the Germans, was the capital of the Austro-Hungarian province then known as Galicia, which on modern maps is called the West Ukraine. With several neighboring dioceses situated to the south, which were under Hungarian rule, Galicia was then the only remaining part of the world the majority of whose population was Catholic of the Slav-Byzantine rite. The priests and the faithful belonged to the Catholic Church, while celebrating their religious services according to the same rite as the Orthodox churches of Russia and in the same language: liturgical Slavonic.

For the past eighteen months, since January 12, 1901, the Metropolitan of Lvov had been Bishop Andrew Sheptitzky. His ancestors, the Sheptitzky counts, had formerly belonged to the community of the Byzantine rite. Afterward, they had

become more and more Polish in their ways and had adopted
the Latin rite through a kind of snobbishness not infrequent
among the nobility. Indeed, the Latin clergy was considered
more cultivated than the clergy of the Byzantine rite. Young
Count Andrew Sheptitzky had therefore been baptized according to the Latin rite. However, when he decided to become a monk and a priest, he returned to his ancestral rite
in order to be closer to his people. This gesture was all the
more praiseworthy as, in order to accomplish it, he had to
overcome his father's energetic opposition. Hoping to discourage him, his family, before giving him permission to
enter the novitiate of the Basilian monks, had obliged him
first of all to finish his law studies at the University of Cracow.

To be more certain of obtaining a scholarship in Rome,
young Feodorov needed the recommendation of some personage of influence. He could not ask this of any of the
Polish bishops established in Russia without compromising them with the Russian government. But the rare Russian Catholics then living in St. Petersburg were well informed of the interest which Metropolitan Andrew felt in
anything which could favor the reconciliation of Russia and
the Holy See. Leonid and his guide therefore decided to
knock at his door.[1]

On the fringes of the Catholics of the Latin rite, who
were of foreign origin, a tiny circle of Catholics of authentic
Russian extraction was being formed in the capital and several other Russian cities despite the stringent laws against
them. In general, they were friends and disciples of Princess
Elizabeth Volkonsky and of Vladimir Soloviov. The most
active member of the group was Miss Natalie Sergueievna
Ushakov. Less inclined to contemplation than her good
friend, Princess Volkonsky, she had, on the other hand, a
well-developed sense of action and organization. She en-

joyed the friendship of the Dowager Empress Marie Feo-
dorovna, widow of Czar Alexander III; she had the privilege
of entrance to the government ministries, and it was especially easy for her to see the Procurator General of the
Holy Synod, Konstantin Pobyedonovtzev. Thus more than
once she was able to help other Catholics who came to be
in a difficult position.

As a whole, the Catholic clergy of the Latin rite who were
living in the Russian Empire had but little desire to protect
any of these Russians of old extraction who had become
Catholics. By looking after a few isolated cases, the clergy
risked incurring the displeasure of the government and, by
that very fact, compromising all their own pastoral activity
among hundreds of thousands of Catholics established from
St. Petersburg to Vladivostok. Furthermore, this body of
Catholic clergy was composed above all of Poles who tradi-
tionally associated Catholicism with the Roman rite. By a
reflex common to all minority ethnic groups submerged in
the midst of a much larger population tending to assimilate
them, they felt very much attached to their own rite, which
distinguished them from the other Christians of the Empire.
Is it necessary to add that the memory of the partition of their
Polish fatherland by its three powerful neighbors, of its efforts
to regain its independence and the repressions which had
followed, remained after all deep in their hearts, and prevented them from feeling the same emotions as these ardent
Russian patriots who had become Catholics. Thus the little
circle of St. Petersburg turned toward the young Metropolitan
of Lvov.

When Father Stislavsky and young Feodorov called on
him in Lvov on a summer's day of 1902, Metropolitan
Andrew had been in possession of his see for only a little over
a year. They were able to stay with him a whole week with-

out any difficulty. On their departure, Bishop Sheptitzky gave them a letter which was to introduce and recommend them to Pope Leo XIII.

Several days later, the two travelers from St. Petersburg reached the heart of the Catholic world; they were able to kneel beside the tombs of the holy Apostles Peter and Paul and to visit the Catacombs and other Roman shrines. The last day of July was the feast of St. Ignatius Loyola, the date chosen for Leonid's definitive entry into the Catholic Church. He went to the Church of the Gesù, and there before the altar where the relics of the saint are kept, he confessed his sins, read his profession of Catholic faith to Father Stislavsky, and received holy Communion.

Shortly afterward, Pope Leo XIII received the two travelers in a private audience. Father Stislavsky gave the Holy Father the letter which the Metropolitan of Lvov had written him; he introduced his young traveling companion and informed the Pope of Leonid's desire to continue preparing himself for the priesthood in Italy. Russian pilgrims were rare in Rome in comparison with those of countries closer to Italy, and the case of this young man who had left his homeland at the price of so many sacrifices was indeed exceptional. Therefore, the Holy Father gave him special and very paternal attention; he blessed him and encouraged him as best he could. The Pope had just founded a new regional seminary at Anagni, about thirty miles south of Rome. He sent Leonid there, and gave him a scholarship to complete his studies for the priesthood.

Because of the great number of dioceses in Central Italy, they were usually too small and too poor to maintain separate seminaries. To obviate this difficulty and to provide sound training for the clergy, the Holy See had for the past few years been organizing regional seminaries for the purpose of grouping the seminarians from several dioceses. Anagni's seminary was such an institute and bore the name "Leonianum" for the Pope who had founded it. Placed under the direction of the Fathers of the Society of Jesus, its student body was composed mainly of seminarians from southern Latium.* Father Stislavsky escorted Leonid to Anagni on October 20, 1902, and then returned to his parish in St. Petersburg. It had been agreed, so as not to attract the attention of Russian postal authorities and police, that the new seminarian was to assume in Italy the name of Leonidas Pierre.

Anagni, famous since Nogaret's assault on Pope Boniface VIII in 1303, is at an altitude of about 1500 feet. The town suffers long and severe winters, and at the seminary prayer and study always took place in unheated rooms floored with hard, cold tile. The young Italians made the best of it. Seated at their worktables, they buried themselves in sweaters and coats and waited out each day to find a little warmth at nightfall beneath their blankets.

But Leonid could not help dreaming nostalgically of the pleasant evenings at St. Petersburg spent by the fire while the wind whistled outside. . . . In the refectory, macaroni and spaghetti, dried beans and chick peas alternated invariably on the plates, and at the beginning of his stay, Madame Feodorov's son often thought of the tasty dishes which far beyond the Alps, on the banks of the Neva, his mother was preparing for the faithful patrons of the *Malii Yaroslavietz.* . . . Leonid was twenty-three, whereas most of his classmates were five and even six years younger. Their youth, their southern exuberance, quite annoyed him at times, but he was good-natured and fell into step with them without grumbling.

His knowledge of Latin helped him learn Italian in no

* The outlying districts of Rome.

time at all, and according to his former classmates, he learned
it perfectly. When he spoke, he could soon be taken for a
fellow countryman of Dante and Manzoni.

With the best will possible, he abided to the last detail
by rules that were all new to him. In sirocco country, the
noon siesta is obligatory for young and old alike. The practice
appears on the seminary schedule as *"riposo a tavola"*—rest
at table. The seminarian is supposed to be seated and to drop
his head on his arms, crossed on the table before him.
Leonid, however, who had never seen anything of the like,
interpreted this in his own way. Each noon, with tireless
patience, he removed books, papers, and inkwells from his
worktable and lay down on it lengthwise throughout the time
prescribed. One day a classmate saw him while he was in
that position, and the news created such a sensation that it
was still remembered forty years later. All the young men
took great interest in Leonid and felt much drawn to him
because of his kind and obliging manners. They were aware
of the reasons for his exile, and in that milieu, where generosity in God's service was highly valued, the young Russian
found himself admired and haloed almost as a confessor of
the faith.

Leonid soon took advantage of the curiosity that his
presence had aroused to acquaint his comrades with religious
problems in Russia. He became fast friends with one who was
later to become the Bishop of Anagni, Mgr. Attilio Adinolfi.
Leonid told him of his hopes and plans. He was convinced
that this young cleric, whose qualities had already been re-
marked by his companions, would one day exert at Rome an
influence greater than the others, and he wanted him to
champion the interests of Russia. "Russia is so ill known in
Rome," he repeated. "Russia actually is so much closer to
Rome than the Protestant countries, but any error in her

regard can cause a very serious prejudice to the cause of Re-
union . . ." Leonid even awoke a particular interest in
Russia in one of his professors, a Frenchman, Father Louis
Baile. It was he who, with Father Alexander Sipiaguine, a
Russian priest, was to found fifteen years later, a boarding
school at Constantinople for boy emigrants from Russia.
This institution, called St. George's Boarding School, was
transferred subsequently to Belgium, then to France.[2]

Getting used to the studies was not easy for Leonid at
Anagni. The philosophy courses, given in Latin and according to scholastic methods, baffled him at first. Moreover, the
curriculum included mathematics, which he had dropped
four years before, and for which he had never much cared
in any case. Throughout the two years he had to study the
subject, it was a perpetual struggle for him to follow the
professor, and on the eve of his final examination in mathematics he spent the entire night trying to prepare himself.
Once he had somehow managed to complete the test, he
rushed to his professor, Father Sinibaldi, dropped on his desk
the algebra and trigonometry manuals that he had been lent,
and sighed, "Thank God, Father, it's over! Here are your
books, and God help me to forget it all!" On the other hand,
he was greatly interested in natural sciences, whose utility
in apologetics he recognized.

A year after his arrival at the seminary, the illness and
later the death of Pope Leo XIII for a time diverted his attention from his studies. He obtained permission to go to
Rome, and on August 4, 1903, he was at St. Peter's to receive
the first blessing of the new Pope, Pius X.

After three years of philosophy, Seminarian Leonidas
Pierre, whose progress had been constant, finally received,
according to the custom of the seminary at that time, the
degree of doctor of philosophy, together with the distinguish-

ing marks that accompanied it; that is, the ring and the four-cornered biretta. After the vacation he began the study of theology, which was to prepare him more directly for the priesthood. A few notebooks carefully preserved by his friend Mgr. Adinolfi attest to his application. In these pages, filled with a firm, regular handwriting, he grouped numerous Greek, Latin, and Russian quotations which he had selected from his reading of the Fathers and the Acts of the Councils. "My years of study, especially those at Anagni," he was to write later, "were a genuine revelation to me. The austere life, the regularity, the rational and intensive work demanded of me, my companions who were full of joy and spirit and not yet corrupted by the atheistic writings of the times; the Italian people themselves, so alive, so intelligent and so imbued with true Christian civilization—all that put me back on my feet and instilled a new energy in me. . . . The Byzantine condescension and passiveness in the face of evil," he went on, "gave way in me to the noble Roman outlook: 'Perat mundus, fiat iustitia!' ('Even if the world should perish, let justice be done!')."

"At the Anagni seminary," he tells us further, "I learned to love the people, and more particularly, our Russian people. I felt a compelling need to do something for the poor and humble Russian people, the ascetic people. . . . Above all, I became aware of the inequality in the Catholic Church of the different rites, and my soul reacted against the injustice of the Latins toward the Orientals, against their general ignorance of Oriental spiritual culture." [3]

Since the breach of unity between Rome and Byzantium, the majority of Catholics have resided in countries formerly evangelized by missionaries from Rome. As a result, those Catholics have inherited the language and liturgical customs as well as the Roman ecclesiastical discipline; the Roman way of approaching theological and ascetic problems; in other words, what is usually called the Latin rite.* It is doubtless inevitable that for many minds this factual situation should gradually appear to be a legal one, whereas in this they are mistaken.

It is certain that in order to complete the social structure of His Church and guarantee to a greater degree its unity and independence vis-à-vis the States of this world, Christ bestowed a superior pastoral mission upon His Apostle Peter. Peter died in Rome, and each Bishop of Rome who has succeeded him over the centuries finds himself vested with this supreme mission. Despite this special function entrusted to the Bishop of Rome by virtue of divine institution, it cannot be concluded that the liturgical and canonical customs of Rome that have grown from human contingencies should be considered by the Church superior to those of other Christian regions. "The Church of Jesus Christ," Pius XI was to write twenty years later "is neither Latin nor Greek nor Slav; it is Catholic. Between its sons, there is no difference. Whether Latin, Greek, Slav, or from other nations, all enjoy the same rights in the eyes of the Apostolic See." [4]

Actually, however, this concept of the equality of rites in the Church has been a blur in the minds of many who nevertheless have believed themselves Catholic. As we have seen, after their conquest of the Christian Near East, the Crusaders established there, in the place of, or side by side with the former Oriental hierarchies, a hierarchy of Latin bishops and after the wanton destruction of the city, they even placed a Latin patriarch in the chair of Constantinople. They brought to the East, therefore, an unjustifiable superi-

---

* Following the current usage, Leonid Feodorov was always to speak of the *Latin* rite. To be precise, one should speak of the *Roman* rite. It is known that certain very old dioceses, such as those at Milan and Lyons, and certain monks, such as the Carthusian and Dominican Orders, although they employ Latin as a liturgical language, conduct their religious services according to rites different from those at Rome.

ority complex which was to spread to the rest of the Catholic world. In the minds of many Polish Catholic priests, just as in those of many Latin missionaries in the Orient, the Latin rite was considered *the* Catholic rite. Others were only temporarily tolerated pending the uniform adoption of the Latin rite.

"Father Stislavsky," Leonid liked to relate, "the good Pole that he was, had insisted at the time I entered the seminary that I adopt the Latin rite. Being timid and still young in the Catholic Church, I did not decline so as not to vex him. However, after several weeks at the Leonianum, in meditating on Metropolitan Sheptitzky's instructions, I realized that my true duty as a Catholic was, on the contrary, to remain steadfast to the Russian rite and traditions. The Sovereign Pontiff very definitely desired this. Those who interpreted his formal directives differently were obviously blinded by their nationalism and lacked a genuinely Catholic sense." [5]

The fact that Leonid enjoyed describing to his companions the splendor of the Russian ceremonies or singing hymns in the solitude of his cell, did not mean that he was narrow or sectarian. On the contrary, he was interested in good wherever he found it. When a Marian sodality was formed at the seminary in order to stimulate the students' devotion to the Blessed Virgin, Leonid became a very active member.

The discovery of unevangelized lands in America, Asia, Africa and Oceania; the triumph of Protestantism in a number of countries; the opposition between Church and State since the French Revolution, and the extension of secularism have led the Western Church throughout the past four centuries to take many initiatives in the field of religious studies, the formation of elite groups, the missionary apostolate, educational institutions and aid to the underprivileged. Leonid studied all these developments. The entire history and life of the Church enthralled him. However, he preferred the Oriental approach and customs. When he was advised to travel during the vacation period to relax a bit, he would go to the Greek monastery of Grottaferata, near Rome, or to the country home of the Greek College at Rieti, so as to establish ties of friendship with the Roman Orientalists of the day.

CHAPTER FOUR

Events in Russia, 1904–1907

WHILE Leonid was preparing for the priesthood in his retreat
at Anagni, Russia was the scene of portentous military and
political happenings. A year and a half after his arrival in
Italy, on the night of February 8 to 9, 1904, Japanese torpedo-
boats launched a sudden attack on the Russian Pacific fleet
off Port Arthur and inflicted upon it very serious losses. An
exhausting war between the two countries followed. On
January 2, 1905, Port Arthur capitulated after resisting a
seven months' siege, and the whole of Russia went into
mourning.

Leonid was kept informed of events continuously through
his mother's letters, and he shared the emotion that was felt
in St. Petersburg. "I was convinced that Port Arthur would
not be able to resist the siege," his mother wrote, "but the
news of its capture nonetheless had such a deep effect on me
and on our old servant that the lunch we had prepared was
left untouched. The next day we reheated it, but again we did
not eat it. In the kitchen someone asked the servant: 'Why
haven't you washed the dishes for two days? Are you fasting?'

No one guessed the real reason except a Polish woman who answered: 'It's not Lent which has taken away their appetite, but Port Arthur!' Altogether during the past two days we have eaten only a smoked herring. . . ." [1]

During the year 1905, Leonid learned of the defeats of the Russian army in Manchuria. Russia's hopes were now fixed on her Baltic fleet, which in October 1904 had sailed for the Far East under the command of Admiral Rojdestvensky. At the end of May 1905, Leonid learned from the newspapers that it had been completely destroyed at Tsu-Shima.

The war against Japan also took a disastrous turn in distant Korea, while at home in Russia those intellectuals who opposed the autocracy of the Emperor for the first time united with the masses to press their claims. Never had St. Petersburg known such feverish unrest; the one subject of conversation was the concessions to be forced from Czar Nicholas II.

"I am very happy that you are not with us in all this disturbance," Madame Feodorov wrote her son, "not because I would be afraid for you, but because your studies would suffer. Here at home it is impossible at the moment to work even in one's room. The temptation to read the newspapers is irresistible, and once one has picked them up one's brain begins to work, worrying over the question 'What really is the truth?'. . . I have kept all the newspapers on the Duma for you; perhaps you would like me to send them to you. I still have the habit of telling you about everything; I have this always on my mind and am constantly afraid that I might forget something. Were it not for this, I would no doubt have put aside all these stupid worldly preoccupations long ago. Perhaps, and even probably, you are not interested in them either. Too bad—I want you to know everything. My Greek blood is boiling; my heart beats faster when I think of my country. Indeed, we are no longer of this world, but important spiritual issues are at stake; the Church of Christ is in danger. The reason is that the people have turned away from the popes [Russian priests], and ask: 'How can we respect priests who incite wrongdoers against the people?' The bishops in particular will have to answer for their complacency toward the civil authorities. . . ." [2]

In January 1905, one industrial strike succeeded another. On Sunday the 22nd, which is commemorated by the name 'Red Sunday,' a procession of thousands of workers carrying icons and portraits of the Czar marched to the Winter Palace to hand a petition to the sovereign. They were greeted with shots, and hundreds of them fell. The effect of this was to give still more impetus to the tide of revolution. On October 17 (October 30 by the Gregorian calendar *) Czar Nicholas II was finally obliged to sign the manifesto which, among other concessions, allowed his people freedom of worship, of meeting, of association, and equality before the law of all citizens whatever their religious beliefs or their origin.

God knows with what impatience Catholic Russians had waited to be granted this freedom of worship! For fifty years a Russian elite—the Swetchines, Golitzines, and Martinovs, the Gagarines, the Chuvalovs and many others—had been obliged to go into voluntary exile from the Empire so that they could belong to the Church which they firmly believed to represent Christ's purposes. Others were forced into silence and hiding. They were filled with joy at the thought that they could at last serve God inside Russia without hindrance and as their consciences directed them.

The intrepid Miss Ushakov immediately set to work. In her villa in Bieloostrov, a short distance from the frontier of Finland, she had given shelter to Father Alexis Zerchaninov,[3] who had come there five years before from the distant Gov-

* Since the beginning of the twentieth century the Julian calendar, which survived in Russia, has been 13 days behind the Gregorian calendar.

ernment of Nizhni-Novgorod. Father Alexis had formerly belonged to the eparchy or Orthodox diocese of that province.
His bishop had appointed him to the parish of the village
of Borissovo, of which half of the inhabitants adhered to the
"Old Believers," a sect which in the seventeenth century had
become separated from the Russian national Church after a
revision of the liturgical books. To bring the dissenters into
the Orthodox Church, Father Alexis buried himself in the
study of the Church Fathers and the history of the Ecumenical
Councils. His research brought him to a conclusion different
from the one he had first sought: he became convinced that
only the Roman Church corresponded to the traditions of the
first centuries. Indeed, he became Catholic before he had ever
met a Catholic priest. A plain-spoken man, sometimes even
rather crude, he made no secret of his convictions and soon
had to pay the price for this: he was arrested and imprisoned
in Suzdal in a place of confinement for bad priests. He spent
two years there, deprived of the exercise of his priestly functions. Like all Orthodox diocesan priests in Russia, Father
Alexis was married. His wife left him and adopted the position of a priest's widow; only one of his children, his oldest
son, followed him. Fortunately, Miss Ushakov was informed
of his misfortune; she set her heart on obtaining his liberation and skillfully exerted her influence on Mr. Pobyedonovtzev, Procurator General of the Holy Synod, in his favor.
In 1900, Father Zerchaninov was able to end his involuntary
seclusion and go and live in the country house which Miss
Ushakov owned near the Finnish border.

After the manifesto of October 17, 1905, she brought
Father Alexis into the capital, where he rented a room at
No. 12 Polozovaya Street, the house of a Russian Catholic,
Madame Timofeiev. He made it into a chapel and cautiously
began to celebrate the Divine Eucharistic Liturgy * there. A

* The Mass in the Eastern Church.

few Russian Catholics came to attend, and in this way a Russian Catholic parish came into being.

Some months later, another priest, Father John Deibner, came from the Government of Tobolsk in Siberia to join him. An ardent disciple of Vladimir Soloviov, he had secretly become a Catholic in 1899, and three years later had been ordained by Metropolitan Andrew. He was then an official in the Government of Saratov, and at the time of the manifesto of October 17 he was a district commissar in Siberia. Immediately he requested and obtained his transfer to St. Petersburg.

Nonetheless, the position of the new parish, and particularly that of Father Zerchaninov, was very precarious. It is true that after October 17 any Russian could become Catholic provided he complied with certain formalities. On the borders of Russia and Poland, thousands of former Catholics who had been forced into the Orthodox Church in 1875 took advantage of their liberty in order to return to the Catholic Church. But all of them were obliged to go over to the Latin rite, since the government was categorically opposed to the building of Catholic churches of Byzantine rite. Prince Peter Volkonsky sadly wrote: "It was legal in Russia to build mosques, Buddhist pagodas, Protestant chapels of every sort, a whole series of Masonic lodges, and even Catholic churches of Latin rite, but a Catholic church of Byzantine rite—never! It would have had too great an attraction!" [4]

We may perhaps agree with Prince Peter Volkonsky in believing that the Czarist government was afraid that too many people would be converted to Catholicism, but its opposition to any sort of Catholic activity in the Byzantine rite stemmed from deeper reasons which are difficult to describe with precision.

Latin Catholics in general feel no emotional repugnance in recognizing the primacy in the Church of the Bishop of

Rome; indeed their sense of history inclines them to consider Rome as the center of the Christian world. From Ireland
to Poland and from Portugal to Hungary, the faithful know
that the Christian message was once brought to them by
missionaries from Rome, and even today they pray together
according to the Roman rite and in what was once the language of Rome. When they go in pilgrimage to what they like
to call the "Eternal City," they are moved at finding there
things which remind them not only of the chief Apostles
but also of outstanding popes, of the founders of religious
Orders, and of numerous saints and doctors of the Church.

For the Russians, on the other hand, this cannot be true.
They know that they became Christians without the intermediary of Rome, and some would not even hesitate to say
that it was *in spite of* Rome that they are Christians, in the
sense that, through their intrigues and their armed aggres-
sion, Russia's Catholic neighbors have often put its religion
in danger. Most often these empirical and temporal considerations outweigh truly religious and dogmatic ones.

Moreover, in the same way as the Greek accepted Christianity with the mentality of a philosopher and the Latin
with his love of clarity and justice, so the Russian received
it with his own particular genius, which is first and foremost
aesthetic. Thus Russian Christianity has a character which is
peculiar to it, and which appears as much in the life of
society as in that of individuals, and the deepest expression
of which is to be found in the *rite,* in the widest sense of the
term. In this way the Russian-Byzantine rite has become for
Orthodox Russians a sort of inalienable family heritage.
Nothing could prevent Lutherans, Muslims, and even, in
some circumstances, Latin Catholics, from living in Russia—
and indeed this had little importance, for their way of praying showed at once that they were foreigners. But what
seemed inacceptable was that a denomination having no ties

with the Russian nation, and even, as some thought, hostile to it, should try to take over what was essentially Russian, and so threaten to divide the country.

Because of these deep-rooted prejudices, the position of Father Zerchaninov and his little chapel in St. Petersburg was highly insecure. All his rights had been taken away from him when he became a Catholic, and he had been forbidden to live in the capital for a period of seven years. For this reason he constantly risked arrest and, at the least, removal to the provinces. But Miss Ushakov's prestige served as a shield for him. She was not only a close relative, but had been for a long time a friend of the Minister of the Interior, Peter A. Stolypin, also president of the Council of Ministers. Insistently she attempted to have Father Zerchaninov and the young Catholic community officially recognized, making appeal to the edict of toleration granted in 1905. Each time the only reply she received was the same declaration from the minister: "Live as you live now; act as you are acting at present; we will close our eyes. But as for granting official recognition of your existence, that is impossible!"

In the spring of 1907, Miss Ushakov obtained permission for Father Alexis to go abroad. She wanted him to make contact with Catholic circles in Europe, to broaden his outlook and make him more competent to direct his growing parish.

His first stop was at Lvov, where he was the guest of Metropolitan Andrew. When he reached Rome, Leonid came from Anagni to act as his interpreter and guide.

Pope Pius X granted Father Alexis a private audience and confirmed all the points of the program of action for Russian Catholics. "The Holy Church," he assured the pilgrim, "will be very reluctant to allow a member of the Eastern Church to go over to the Latin rite."

"When the time came to leave," Leonid notes in a letter of the period,[5] "His Holiness handed Father Alexis two medals bearing his image and gave him his blessing. Father Zerchaninov was most enthusiastic about the audience and very moved at being greeted with such kindness and simplicity."

"During his stay in Rome," Leonid adds, "I questioned him extensively about the situation of Catholics in Russia. I was able to ascertain that he is really one of us (it had been rumored that he wanted to go over to the Latin rite). His drawback is that he is somewhat eccentric and lacks any sort of systematic scientific education."

Leonid ended the letter with this news: "The affair of my belonging to the Byzantine rite has been settled in the best possible way: '*Sanctitas sua benigne annuit juxta preces . . . contrariis quibuscumque non obstantibus.*' * In this way (by this pontifical decree) I have been recognized as an Eastern Catholic by right and in fact. I belong to the Latin rite as a purely temporary measure."

This decree of the Holy Father which fifty years later will surprise no one, and even seems normal, represented in its time a courageous stand, a turning point in the apostolic activity of the Catholic Church on behalf of Russia.

To understand it, we must again take up the Polish problem, this time in greater detail. At the end of the eighteenth century, Poland, although still forming a distinct nation from the ethnic, linguistic and political point of view, was progressively divided and absorbed by its three power neighbors, Prussia, Austria and Russia. The last of these had taken the largest part of the country and had begun a process of Russification which, to begin with, was fairly mild.

But the Polish people, undoubtedly the most chivalrous in the world, was never to lose its national feeling and its de-

---

* Leonid had sent a letter to the Holy See begging to be officially recognized as a Catholic of the Byzantine rite. Here he quotes the first and the last words of the Latin answer which he received: "The Holy Father has favorably agreed to your request . . . whatever may be the objections."

sire for independence. In 1830, influenced by the revolutionary spirit that was rising elsewhere in Europe, it staged its first insurrection, which was crushed by force. In 1863 a new uprising lasted several months before it was repressed by Russian troops, and feeling in Europe was incited against Russia. Reprisals were more severe than ever; thousands of Poles were executed or deported to European and Asiatic Russia, and the Russification of the country was undertaken with still greater intensity.

In order to preserve their national identity, the Poles who had been dispersed to the four corners of the Empire clung obstinately to the things that distinguished them from the Russian surroundings into which they had been thrown: their language and, above all, their religion. The Orthodox religion of the Russians and the Catholicism of the Poles do not differ very widely in their fundamental dogmas, but the external forms of worship are quite characteristic and distinguish one from the other very clearly. They became a symbol of nationality and of opposition.

It is easy to see what could have been the consequences of this situation: if those Russians who believed themselves to be bound in conscience to recognize the primacy of the Bishop of Rome had been forced to follow the Latin rite, they would in fact have strengthened the Polish minority and represented a conquest and a victory for it. On the other hand, the development of Catholicism of Byzantine rite represented a danger for this minority, for it would certainly attract young Poles who wanted to be absorbed into the Russian people without giving up their Catholic beliefs. By keeping the young Russian Feodorov in the Byzantine rite the Holy See took up a stand in the conflict and, looking beyond Polish aspirations, gave the only truly Catholic solution to the problem. But this solution would not be understood or accepted in St. Petersburg without lengthy opposition.

The pastor of St. Catherine's, Father Stislavsky, especially showed the greatest disappointment when he learned that his pupil had decided to be ordained in the Byzantine rite. The letter which he sent Leonid still exists. "True Russians," he wrote to the seminarian in his annoyance, "feel the greatest repulsion for everything that suggests Byzantianism and the Tartars. The Eastern rite has become so discredited in their view that they will not hear of anything that comes from Byzantium. Only those who are as ignorant of the life of the people as our French friends, see everything back to front. The Russians want nothing to do with this Eastern rite which is associated with everything disgusting and retrograde in Russia." [6] The Frenchmen referred to in this letter are the Dominican and Assumptionist priests settled in St. Petersburg who gave whole-hearted support to Miss Ushakov and her friends of the Russian Catholic community.

The pastor of St. Catherine's did not confine himself to words; in his vexation he decided to cut off his unfaithful disciple's livelihood. In the past he had sent Leonid a small but regular allowance. Going back on his express promises, he let him know that henceforth his own resources would be low, and he could no longer do anything for him.

Leonid did not protest nor change his mind for so little. But this lack of money came at an inconvenient time. The seminarian just happened to have obtained permission from his superiors at the Anagni seminary to go during the approaching summer holidays of 1907 to the first Congress of Velehrad in Moravia. Theologians who specialized in Eastern questions were to meet there to study together the problem of reestablishing the unity of the Eastern and Western Churches. From Velehrad, Leonid hoped to be able to go to Lvov and spend a few days with Metropolitan Andrew. He told the Metropolitan of his misfortune; the necessary money was sent him and he was in a position to carry out his plan.

However, before he could set out for the Congress in Moravia something happened which was to force him to abandon any hope of return to the Seminary of Anagni and the many friends he had made there.

CHAPTER FIVE

Distress in America
Feodorov's Efforts in Rome

FOR five years Leonid had lived peacefully at the Leonianum, and no one had ever troubled him. The Russian government seemed to have lost interest in his fate. Eventually, however, it was obliged to draw its attention back to him, for the passport which he had obtained in St. Petersburg was about to expire. One morning in the summer of 1907 he went to Rome and requested the Russian Imperial Legation to the Holy See to grant its renewal. A preemptory reply was not long in coming: "If Leonid Feodorov does not leave at once an establishment directed by the Jesuits, he will be forbidden ever again to return to Russia."

Leonid could not conceive any field of action for his work as a priest other than Russia, so he decided to comply with the order he had received. He would finish his theological studies in Rome, at the Urban College of the Propaganda, a Pontifical college which admitted seminarians from the various countries of the world which had as yet been unable to organize their own seminaries in Rome. In the meantime he proceeded to the Congress at Velehrad.

Leonid's part in the Congress was discreet; he was too young a theologian to get up and speak, so he contented himself with listening, asking questions and trying above all to form bonds of friendship with the assembled ecumenicists which later on might be useful to him. That he aroused confidence in those whom he met is proved by the fact that he returned to Italy bringing with him an urgent appeal to the Holy See from the Eastern Catholics of the United States. Even before transferring his belongings from Anagni to the College of the Propaganda, he went to knock at the door of some of the most influential of the Roman cardinals. The situation he sought to make clear was the following:

Toward the end of the nineteenth century and at the beginning of the twentieth, hundreds of thousands of immigrants, flooding from the Eastern regions of the Austro-Hungarian Empire, had emigrated to the United States. As they were very poor, they were glad to accept the hardest of jobs, first of all on farms in New England, then in the ports of New York and Philadelphia, and later in the coal mines of Pennsylvania. Without any pretensions, often even illiterate, these hardy people who had come from territories where the upper classes had received their education in Polish, German or Hungarian, did not claim a common nationality, although they all spoke more or less the same language. Some called themselves Galicians, others said they were Ruthenians, Hungarians, Slovaks or Ukrainians. In fact, one term alone covered them all: they were *Greek Catholics*. This meant that they were united with Rome, but their priests celebrated the services in the Slavonic tongue and kept the Byzantine liturgical tradition.

In 1884 several of these immigrants sent a petition from Shenandoah, Pennsylvania, to Archbishop Sylvester Sembratovich, predecessor of Metropolitan Andrew Sheptitzky in the see of Lvov. In their letter, touching in its faith and simplicity, they asked the Metropolitan to send them pastors of their own rite. The first priest arrived in November of that same year, Father Ivan Volansky, a very zealous man and an excellent organizer. He immediately built a church in Shenandoah, and organized a parish, a choir, a library and a dramatic group. By the end of the century, about forty other Catholic priests of the Greek rite had followed him to the New World.[1]

At this time the Catholic Church of the Latin rite in the United States was fully organized and on the eve of a period of great expansion. The bishops were laboring in all possible ways to ensure the perseverance in the faith of the Irish, German, Polish, Slovak and other Catholics who were arriving in great numbers in a country where Protestants were in the dominant majority. Some of these Catholics—particularly the Germans in the Midwest—tended to keep their own language and cultural traditions and to constitute separate groups opposed to assimilation in the vast American melting-pot. The most farsighted American bishops, on the other hand, wanted the Catholic Church to become fully American as quickly as possible.

It is not difficult to understand that the arrival of these Eastern rite Catholics complicated the situation still more. They were so different from all the others! They did not want their services to be celebrated in Latin, but in Slavonic. They received the sacrament of Confirmation, not from their bishop, but from their parish priests. Moreover, most of their priests were married.

In the West very early the Church began to urge celibacy on her priests to help them identify themselves more closely with Christ and dedicate themselves more freely to their spiritual duties. On the other hand, in the East, among

Catholics as well as non-Catholics, celibacy is required only of monks and bishops. Although a priest may never marry, a married man may be ordained a priest. As a matter of fact, at that time most of the diocesan priests among the Greek Catholics were married.

The presence of married priests in a country where all other Catholic priests were celibate raised, of course, a delicate problem. Upon landing in Philadelphia, the first act of Father Volansky had been to present himself to the Latin Ordinary, Archbishop Patrick Ryan. When the prelate learned that he was a married man, he refused him jurisdiction. Father Volansky sent a telegram to Archbishop Sembratovich to ask whether he could fulfill his obligations without the approval of the local Latin rite Ordinary. Receiving no answer either to act or not to act, he had started organizing his parish in Shenandoah.

The first Greek Catholic priests who followed Father Volansky considered themselves to be under the jurisdiction of the bishops of Eastern Europe who had sent them. Obviously, this situation could not continue indefinitely. The American bishops intervened and conflicts arose. Trying to put order into the situation, the Holy See promulgated in 1890 a decree which, among other things, proclaimed the exclusive jurisdiction of the Latin bishops over the Greek Catholics of the United States, and compelled their married priests already established in America to return to Europe. The energetic pioneer Father Volansky had to abandon his flock and go to Brazil, leaving behind a great void and also much bitterness.

That same year a painful incident occurred in Minneapolis. A priest who had recently arrived from the Diocese of Presov, Slovakia, Father Alexis Toth, a widower, went to pay a visit to Archbishop John Ireland of St. Paul, Minnesota. He explained that he had been invited by the Greek Catholics of Minneapolis to organize a parish of their rite. But the Archbishop refused permission and denied him jurisdiction. Exactly what took place between the Archbishop and Father Toth is difficult to say with objectivity.* Their conversation had no witness, and is reported in different ways by the friends and the opponents of the Archbishop. At any rate, when Father Toth came back to the Greek Catholic community of Minneapolis and told them of Archbishop Ireland's refusal, they became indignant. These simple people, who were not accustomed to rigid canonical regulations, concluded that they needed a church and a priest of their own rite to provide pastoral and spiritual care. However, a priest must be under a bishop, and if the Latin bishop refused to take their priest under his jurisdiction, there could be only one solution: to send a delegation to the Orthodox bishop of San Francisco, asking him to take them under his protection. Father Toth could still have appealed to the Holy See, but he gave in to his parishioners.

On March 25, 1891, the Orthodox Bishop Vladimir came personally to Minneapolis to receive Father Toth and 361 of his people into the Orthodox Church.

Meanwhile, at the request of the Roman Catholic Archdiocese, a law suit was filed to evict Father Toth from the parish, but its only result was to deepen resentments. By the end of 1898 three other Greek Catholic parishes with their faithful had followed the example of Father Toth. During the following years, the number of these defections increased still further. In 1905 the Orthodox bishop transferred his see from San Francisco to New York to be nearer his new flock.

It was becoming increasingly obvious that the only way

* The long biography of Archbishop John Ireland written by J. H. Monahan does not say a single word about the incident that took place between the Archbishop and Father Toth. This silence seems to indicate that the biographer was unaware of the consequences of the disagreement.

to ease the tension was to give the Greek Catholics of America a bishop of their own rite. Petition after petition for this purpose was sent from America to the Holy See, to the Greek Catholic bishops in Europe, and also to the Austro-Hungarian government; Metropolitan Andrew multiplied his appeals to Rome. As was evident, the problem was not simple: these Eastern rite Catholics had settled in an area where Latin dioceses were already organized. To give them a separate bishop would be to create, to some extent, a state within a state by entrusting the same territory to two different bishops.

Finally, in 1907, the Roman Congregation of the Propaganda had attempted a solution. On March 26 of that year a Basilian priest from Galicia, Father Soter Ortynsky, was appointed first Bishop of the Greek Catholics in the United States. Consecrated on May 12 by Metropolitan Andrew, he arrived in New York on August 27. The general rejoicing, however, was short lived: a month later the Holy See's apostolic letter *Ea Semper* limited considerably the powers of the new bishop, whose center had been established in Philadelphia. He could visit the Greek Catholic parishes only with the approval of the local Latin bishop; he needed the same approval to remove or replace his priests. The Greek Catholic priests were deprived of their right to administer the sacrament of Confirmation and—worse yet—in case of a marriage between Catholics of different rites, the Latin rite enjoyed special privileges.

Very soon it became practically impossible for Bishop Ortynsky to fulfill his duties. While certain Latin bishops were generously trying to assist him in his intricate task, others seemed to ignore him.

When an enterprise is prosperous, its members live in harmony, but in times of distress, when nerves are made tense by contradictions, quarrels easily arise. This was the case with the Greek Catholics. Among them there were two divergent political tendencies—one favorable to Russia, the other favoring the division of Russia and the creation of an independent Ukraine which would have included certain provinces of the Austro-Hungarian Empire in which the Greek Catholics originated. It became extremely difficult for Bishop Ortynsky to keep aloof from these political arguments.

Young Feodorov longed for reconciliation between Russia and the Catholic Church. Hearing at Velehrad about these matters, he understood better than anybody else the new obstacles they would create. Even the higher clergy in the Catholic world did not grasp the full meaning and consequence of events which were taking place in the United States. For three centuries, Greek Catholics had lived under political regimes favorable to the Catholic Church—in Poland, Austria or Hungary. Orthodox writers had been repeating that these people held allegiance to the Catholic Church only because it had been required by the civil powers under which they had lived. The fact that so many of these same people were leaving the Catholic Church once they had arrived in the New World was often cited as proof that these accusations were not without foundation. It is no wonder that the American bishops, who were overwhelmed with their own problems and who never had any contact with the Eastern Christians, did not understand the full meaning of these events, but the Holy See should have opened their eyes to the extent and significance of so many defections.

Leonid decided, therefore, to make every effort to inform the Roman prelates, and if possible to have the Holy See review its decision. He asked for an audience with Cardinals Rampolla and Vives, and he described to them the danger of the situation. The prelates listened attentively. "Both regret deeply," he wrote soon after to Metropolitan Andrew, "that the matter concerning the Bishop of America has taken

such an unfavorable turn. They advise you to write immediately a letter of protest to the Holy Father. It is absolutely
imperative that all the bishops of Galicia, with Your Ex-
cellency at their head, explain to the Holy Father at great
length the situation of the Ruthenian Catholics and their
bishop. You must insist specifically on the danger of schism
and on the discontent of the Ruthenian clergy. This is what
they fear the most here. This letter of protest should be
signed by all the deans, the canons and all the professors
of theology from the seminaries and universities in Galicia.
The same thing must be done in America where all the
Ruthenian priests should sign the document. This letter
of protest should then be sent directly to the Holy Father,
bypassing all intermediaries. This is what the two Cardinals,
as well as the Benedictine Fathers of the Greek College, advised me to do. As far as we can understand, the Roman
prelates dread creating a diocese within a diocese by giving
extended privileges to the Ruthenian bishop. Obviously, they
are completely right in this matter, but they shouldn't go
to the opposite extreme by curtailing so completely the independence of the Ruthenian bishop."

On November 2, 1907, Feodorov made a third visit to
Cardinal Vives to intercede on behalf of the Greek Catholics
of the New World. He then asked for an audience with Cardinal Ledochowski. After this visit he wrote: ". . . His
Eminence has pointed out to me very opportunely that the
Eastern Catholics neglect to provide the Holy See with accurate information about their affairs. The Germans, on the
contrary, inform Rome regularly of their needs and of their
problems, which is greatly to their advantage." [2]

Leonid had clearly foreseen what was going to happen.
Shortly afterward, in the Orthodox world many publications
began referring to the decisions of the Holy See as proof that
the Roman Church would always consider Eastern Christians

as outcasts, and would never sincerely respect their traditions. The newspapers that Leonid received from St. Petersburg kept him informed of the reaction that the Roman decision had provoked in Russia. He patiently translated into Italian the most significant articles so that the cardinals could read them.

Meanwhile in America more Eastern Catholics were leaving the Church, and this trend was to continue. A specialist could write in 1961: "More than four-fifths of the Slavic non-Catholic Eastern Christians in America are former Catholics and their descendants. . . ." *

At the College of the Propaganda, situated on the Piazza di Spagna, right in the heart of Rome, Leonid found himself in a particularly international atmosphere: Japanese and Norwegians, Syrians and New Zealanders rubbed shoulders there, as well as men from many other countries. One of his fellow seminarians had also come from the Russian Empire and was later to become Patriarch of the Armenian Catholics, also Secretary of the Congregation *De Propaganda Fide*. He is now known to us as Cardinal Agagianian.

The time spent in these surroundings gave Leonid a concrete and personal awareness of the universality of the Catholic Church in our time, and of the complexity of modern pastoral problems. From Indians he learned of the problems created by the caste system and of the progress of Islam in Asia, and from Scotsmen of the multiplicity of Protestant sects. In fact, by forcing Feodorov to leave the Leonianum, the Russian government had unintentionally aided the cause of Russian Catholicism. The some thirty miles which separated Anagni and Rome had been enough to prevent Leo-

* Cf. Code of Oriental Canon Law—Persons—Pospishil (St. Mary's Ukrainian Catholic Church, Ford City, Pa., 1960), p. 69. It is generally believed that there would now be at least half a million more Eastern Catholics in the United States if these defections had not taken place.

nid from regular meetings with Russians passing through the
Eternal City, and they had also made it difficult for him to
intercede with the Roman Congregations on behalf of his
friends in St. Petersburg. His presence in Rome made regular
communication with Russia much easier for him.

At this time the situation of the Catholics of Latin rite
scattered throughout the Russian Empire was presenting certain problems for the government. Since in none of the
churches of these Catholics were prayers or sermons given
in Russian—in fact the language of the Catholics in Russia
was Polish—it was becoming increasingly clear that by keeping them in the Latin rite their absorption into the Russian
population was being impeded. The government was naturally interested in having them become fully Russian.

A letter from Leonid to Metropolitan Sheptitzky, dated
November 4, 1907, tells us what the plans of the government
were at this time: "I have been to visit Mr. Sazonov, the
Russian *chargé d'affaires* to the Vatican," he writes.[3] He en-
tertained me most courteously. I stayed with him almost the
whole evening. The conversation returned constantly to ecclesiastical questions, and I came away with the feeling that
the Russian Government is definitely opposed to the idea of
a Catholicism of Byzantine rite. As for the difficulty of satisfy-
ing Russian Catholics, he hopes to overcome it in the following way. He returned to the project of *officia suppletoria.**
Taking as its authority the fact that Poles and Lithuanians
have services of this kind, the Government would like to open
a church of Latin rite in which the sermons and complementary services will be in Russian. In this way, on one hand
it avoids Catholicism of the Byzantine rite, and on the other
provides an alternative to Catholics of Latin rite having to

* Complementary paraliturgical services in the vernacular, which are held
on various occasions and are very popular in Eastern Europe.

adopt the Polish customs and language. It knows quite well that the people—except for some tens of thousands of the faithful in Western Russia—would never consider adhering to the Latin rite, and in this way Orthodoxy would be saved. Still more, the conviction that Catholicism is synonymous with Latin culture would be more and more strongly fixed in the minds of the Russian people, since all Catholics, even those who are not Polish, would be Latin.

"In order to attain this end, the government needs priests who will be able to protect this Latin Church from becoming Polish. Mr. Sazonov has offered me a ready prepared parish if I will agree that I want to become a priest of this type."

If Leonid had had even a slight amount of careerism, the temptation to accept this offer would have been very strong. The total absence of other competitors and the favor which he already enjoyed in Rome as well as that which he would soon have acquired at St. Petersburg, would have opened to him the ranks of the hierarchy. But he seems not even to have considered it, and his letter continues: "I answered [to Mr. Sazonov] that in spite of the complementary services, such a church would still be an element of Polish infiltration because of the strong numerical superiority of the Poles; but he would not believe it."

"If we are to defeat this policy," Leonid concluded, "we must do everything in our power to dissuade Russian priests who go over to Catholicism from adopting the Latin rite. In this way the government will find it impossible to carry out its policy."

While he was taking his third year of theology at the Propaganda, not a month passed without a visit of some friend from Russia. January 1908, the jubilee of St. John Chrysostom, drew a good number of Eastern prelates to Rome. In February, Metropolitan Andrew made a visit *ad limina* to the Vatican. In March, Father Stislavsky arrived in

Italy and told about all the discontent of the Poles in St. Petersburg. At the end of April, Leonid greeted a former member of the Duma, Mr. Alexander Sipyaghin, who had just been received into the Catholic Church, and had come to Rome to prepare himself for the priesthood.

But it was above all Leonid's mother, who had remained in St. Petersburg, who kept him informed of events in the Russian capital. In spite of the length of their separation, the closest bonds continued to exist between mother and son. They wrote to each other often—several times a month. "It seems to me that we understand each other so well," wrote Lyubov Dimitryevna in one of her letters to Leonid, "that even after death you will continue to hear me and you will think in my place. How happy I am that I can die with this thought—that in myself I see you, that in myself I know you." [4]

In 1905, when riots were rocking St. Petersburg, some friends had suggested that she go abroad to live with her son. "For no reason whatsoever would I leave Russia," she wrote them. "I wish to experience everything that my people experience . . . 'Not a hair of your head falls unless the Heavenly Father permits it. . . .' "

Another time some acquaintances were leaving for Italy and asked her for Leonid's address, so that they could visit him. It so happened that at precisely this moment the letters from the seminarian had been less frequent than usual. Lyubov Dimitryevna was going to give them the address, but then changed her mind. "No," she wrote, "I cannot bring myself to do it. Leonid might think that I wish in some way to control him, as if I were doubting his good conduct. I do not wish to break the harmony which exists between us. I have freed him from his filial dependence, and I do not wish to change my decision by asking him why he is silent. He is an honest man and has the right to complete freedom."

CHAPTER SIX

Years of Waiting

On the morning of October 26, 1908, an event of no apparent importance occurred which for a few moments interrupted the regular life of the Albertinum, a college for theological students directed by the Dominican Fathers in Fribourg, Switzerland: the superior, Father Miller, called the seminarians together to present to them a new student who had arrived that night. His name was Antonio Cremoni.

This new candidate for the priesthood was very reserved. However, he was soon thought to be an Italian born in Milwaukee, in the United States, who intended to take up missionary work. Was he not already wearing a curly auburn beard?

In a short time other strange facts about the newcomer appeared. First, he was beginning his fourth year of theology. Where had he studied the three preceding years? Then he showed a marked tendency to seek the company of the thirteen Polish seminarians in the college and to ask them awkward questions about their relations with the Russians. A still more mystifying detail: this odd American received all

58

The end of the academic year 1907–1908 was approac
when suddenly the seminarian Feodorov insisted on ta
his theology examinations before any of his other compan
at the College of the Propaganda. He packed his suitcase, s
good-by to all, giving the impression that he wished to
nounce his ecclesiastical studies and, one fine morning, to
the train for Galicia.

his mail, not from the United States, but from Galicia, and above all from Russia. It was not long before the truth came out and was whispered around: Antonio Cremoni was only a pseudonym; actually the new seminarian was Russian and his real name was Leonid Feodorov.

What had happened, and what was the reason for this peculiar behavior? During his year of theological studies at the College of the Propaganda, Leonid Feodorov had, as we know, on several occasions visited the Russian *chargé d'affaires* to the Vatican, Mr. Sazonov. One day, as the end of the scholastic year was approaching, the Russian diplomat suddenly repeated the threat which he had already made the previous year: "Leonid Ivanovitch," he said, "if you continue to study with the Jesuits, you will be absolutely forbidden to return to Russia. You have been warned!"

"But I have left the Jesuits," Leonid replied. "I am now at the Propaganda College, which is completely independent of the Jesuits."

"Oh—it's the same thing," the diplomat answered. "The spirit there is exactly the same."

Once again Leonid was forced to submit, so shortly afterward he left Rome, and when he went to take his leave of Mr. Sazonov, he told him that he was going to Galicia to act as tutor in a wealthy family. He did indeed go to Galicia for a period of his vacation, but in October he set out for Switzerland so that he could finish his theological studies at the Catholic University of Fribourg. On the way he made a brief stop at Innsbruck, Austria, in order to visit some Russian seminarians, including Father Stanislas Tyszkiewicz, a Jesuit who was later to publish several theological works in Russian.

On his arrival in Fribourg, so as not to attract the attention of the Russian consul, Leonid took the name Antonio Cremoni; and so that he would not have to explain his presence to the Italian consul, who was always on the watch for young

Italians coming to Switzerland to avoid military service, the rumor was spread that Antonio Cremoni came from America.

Later in his life this year of study in Switzerland was to appear to Leonid as above all one of peace and concentrated intellectual work. It also gave him almost a year of practice in speaking French and German. Finally, he liked later to recall the perfect charity which he found at the Albertinum. Even so, a disappointment awaited him at the end of the year. His final examinations had been brilliant, and he had planned to continue his studies for the degree of doctor of divinity, a title which, he thought, would give him a better status with the Polish Catholic clergy in Russia and more independence in his future work. But when he calculated the cost of the examinations and of preparing a thesis, he realized that he was unfortunately too poor to pursue his project.

In the course of the year he had received quite encouraging news from St. Petersburg. First, there was now a third Russian Catholic priest in the capital, Father Eustaphe Sussalev. This priest had been baptized and ordained in the group of the Old Believers; he had asked to be admitted to the Catholic Church, and after enquiry the Holy See had recognized the validity of his ordination.

Meanwhile, the approaches made by Miss Natalie Ushakov to her cousin, Minister Stolypin, to obtain authorization to open a Catholic church of Russian rite, had still produced no results: the minister turned a deaf ear. One day the members of the Russian Catholic community decided to take matters into their own hands. In the upper story of the house in Polozovaya Street, where Father Alexis Zerchaninov lived, they rented a modest apartment composed of three small rooms. One of them became Father Alexis' bedroom and reception room. The wall separating the other two rooms was pulled down, and in the long room so formed, volunteers

fitted out a chapel. They set up a homemade iconostasis *
covered with gilded paper and a very simple altar surmounted
by a tiny tabernacle. In a shop kept by Old Believers, they
bought icons of the Savior and of the Virgin in classical
Russian hieratic style, and Lyubov Dimitryevna Feodorov,
Leonid's mother, undertook to paint the other liturgical
icons in watercolor.

The chapel was ready, but the authorization to celebrate
services there had still not been obtained. So they decided to
carry on without it, and on Easter night, 1909, the three
Russian Catholic priests in St. Petersburg—Fathers Alexis
Zerchaninov, John Deibner and Eustaphe Sussalev—celebrated the Easter service together before quite a large congregation. Immediately after the ceremony they decided to
send a telegram to the Czar, signed by Father Sussalev, who
had until recently been a priest of the Old Believers, with
the following message: "On the joyful feast of the Resurrec-
tion of Christ, the Russian Old Believers in communion with
the Apostolic See of Rome offer to the Almighty their prayers
for the health of Your Imperial Majesty and for that of the
Czarevitch, heir to the throne." A reply soon arrived, signed
by Baron Fredericks, Minister of the Court: "His Majesty
thanks the Old Believers in communion with the Holy See
for their prayers." [1]

Shortly afterward the police, intrigued by the unusually
large number of people who visited the apartment, came to
make enquiries. On being shown the precious telegram, they
left without further questions.

From this time the number of faithful constantly increased,
and the chapel soon became too small. On Sunday during the
Liturgy the last to arrive, unable to get inside the apartment,
filled the staircase and followed the singing and the sermon
as best they could. On these Sundays each of the three priests

* Partition separating the sanctuary from the nave in Byzantine churches.

preached in turn; the sermons of Father Deibner, the most cultured of the three, were particularly well attended.

When Leonid learned of these details in the letters which he received from Russia he was coming to the end of his training for the priesthood, and he ought, in the ordinary way, to have been ordained. He was giving deep thought to this when, at the end of April 1909, he received a long letter from Miss Natalie Ushakov in St. Petersburg.

"For the love of God," she wrote, "do not be ordained a priest. This is the reason: Sazonov [former minister to the Vatican] has told you that he will raise every obstacle he can to the development in Russia of the Eastern Catholic rite. He is influential here; he is Stolypin's brother-in-law, and because of this he could do much harm to you personally and to our cause. As you have a valid passport, return to Russia like any other honest Russian citizen, without being ordained. Gain admittance to the University; prepare the ground. You could talk to young people, and it would be much easier for you to do so as an educated layman than as a Catholic priest. In this case, there would be no deceit; everything would be in order; if you had trouble from the police, it would soon stop. And by thus preparing the ground, you would be of inestimable value.

"On the other hand, if you arrive here after you have been ordained, this is what will happen. In Lvov and throughout Galicia there is a crowd of our secret police. Metropolitan Andrew is very closely watched. You have lived in his house, so you are marked. It will be known at once that you are a priest, and no sooner will you have passed the frontier than you will be followed by the police. You will be accused of tricking people, and you will be told that you are politically undesirable, for otherwise you would not need to hide. The least that could happen to you would be deportation abroad, and you would be lost to our cause.

"Add to this that your activity as a priest could at best be very limited. The public is not used to masquerades. You would sometimes be seen in a cassock and sometimes in a jacket; tongues would begin to wag, and people would say that you were simply an impostor, and that you should not hear confessions. The first gossip would betray you, and the number of gossips is legion.

"Think also of the material situation. We suffer from great material poverty, and however limited your needs, you would nonetheless have to live, eat, drink, and have a roof over your head. Your mother is a blessing to our church and, as you know, she is not rich.

"Excuse me for being so outspoken. When I write: 'Do not be ordained,' I do so only with great reluctance. You cannot know how much I long to have spiritual guidance from an educated Russian priest. To our next meeting, be it sooner or later, as God wishes. May His Will be done in all things." [2]

In these few lines Miss Ushakov had given a very exact picture of the situation. Leonid understood how realistic she was, and he let himself be persuaded. At the beginning of June 1909, he took his final theology examinations, and instead of leaving for Galicia to be ordained, he decided to go to Rome where he would again take up the defense of the Eastern Catholic Church. In the United States, the situation of the Greek Catholic bishop, Soter Ortynsky, had become worse. Confusion reigned in the parishes of his rite, and orders from Rome demanding that the right to administer the sacrament of Confirmation be reserved to bishops alone were not observed; the Greek Catholics went on as they had done in the past, and people left in increasing numbers to join the Orthodox communities.

At the same time slanders which had been invented against Metropolitan Sheptitzky had been given credence by certain influential prelates in the Vatican. As he was eager to en-

courage more and more brotherly relations between Catholic
and Orthodox intellectuals, the Metropolitan had supported
the Congress of Velehrad with every means in his power; he
had also upheld the few Russian priests and laymen who had
wanted to keep their traditional rite when they became
Catholics. The Austrian government had chosen to represent
this as pernicious activity in the cause of Pan-Slavism * and
Russian imperialism. The Metropolitan was thought to be
seeking to dismember the Habsburg Empire by favoring
Slavonic nationalisms.

Two of Leonid's first visits in Rome were to Cardinals
Rampolla and Vives. He realized that these two prelates had
understood Metropolitan Andrew's position and that they
supported his activities.

"All these gentlemen who are in power in the Vatican,"
Leonid objected, "think of our rite as simply tolerated."

"Tolerated!" replied Cardinal Vives. "Of course not: it is
the wish of Holy Mother Church! If you were to come to me
yourself and suggest that I undertake any action against the
Greek rite, I would show you the door!" [3]

So the accusations against Metropolitan Andrew were easily
dispelled. On the other hand, it would still be four years before the limitations placed on the activity of Bishop Ortynsky
would be lifted. Only on May 28, 1913, would the Holy See
finally grant him full ordinary jurisdiction over all Greek
Catholics settled in the United States.

After his visit to Rome, Leonid left for Moravia where the
second Congress of Velehrad was to open in July 1909. During the first Congress, which had assembled two years before
near the tomb of St. Methodius, apostle of the Slavs, 73 members had exchanged their opinions. At this second Congress
there were 168. The Metropolitan of Lvov presided and in

* The Pan-Slav movement of this period was aimed at detaching the Czechs,
Slovaks, Croatians, Slovenes, Poles, and Ukrainians from Austria.

his opening address he stated firmly: "A rumor recently circulated, alas, by the Catholic press, fills me with astonishment. It maintains that our assemblies have been inspired not by a spirit of charity and faith, but as a means to further Pan-Slavism. . . . I affirm that nothing is further from us than the wish to mingle interests and considerations of a political nature to the most holy work of the universality of the faith, and to that of the union of the Churches. . . ." [4]

Once the Congress was over, Leonid made preparations to leave for St. Petersburg. After an absence of seven years, he once again crossed the Russian frontier.

It is not hard to imagine the feelings of his mother, Madame Feodorov, as she waited for her son. Eleven months before, she had also made a profession of Catholic faith. Not long after Leonid's departure for Italy, she came to share and approve the reasons which had made him feel bound in conscience to adhere to the Roman Church. She had become Catholic at heart, but a Latin priest told her that if she wished to be received into the Roman Church she must cease altogether to frequent Orthodox churches. The letter which she wrote to her son at this time gives a vivid picture of the difficulties felt by souls such as hers when they are deprived of the liturgical life in which they have been brought up.

"Although our chapel [that of Father Zerchaninov] fully satisfies me," she wrote, "not many liturgical offices can be celebrated there. However, it was too much for me to stay sitting at home during services. But I made an effort and for a month I did not attend Orthodox services; I began again later and this time I stayed away from them for two months. But this abstention had a disastrous effect on me: I 'melted,' as they say. People asked me: 'Are you ill?' How much my soul suffered from it. . . ."

It was then that Metropolitan Andrew came incognito on a voyage to Russia and called on her to talk to her about her son. "Seeing his angelic kindness," she wrote after this visit, "I felt full of courage and I began to ask him if I could not visit Orthodox churches simply to pray, and not so as to receive unction from the priest on the eve of feasts [unction which is given to the faithful by the priest during the services of matins] or to kiss the cross or the Gospels."

"But," the bishop replied, astonished, "why should you not receive unction from the priest or kiss the cross and the Gospel? All these are holy things. You may go and pray in Orthodox churches." [5]

Leonid's meeting with his mother after seven years' separation was one of the few moments of unmixed human joy in his life. For the little Catholic circle also, Leonid's arrival was a notable event. Everyone felt that he was to be the future pastor of the growing community, and his presence filled them all with new strength, for in addition to the external obstacles imposed on them, there had been no lack of internal difficulties.

The first of these was concerned with the juridical situation of the community. The only Catholic hierarchy which existed in Russia was that of the Polish Latin bishops; because of this, it seemed that Russian Catholics, whatever their origin, should be under their jurisdiction. But to depend in this way on bishops of another rite, and of a different—and even hostile—nationality, would certainly have impeded the young community. So the Russian Catholics had turned to Metropolitan Andrew and asked to be placed under his guidance. How could they justify the intervention of a foreign bishop in Russia? Metropolitan Andrew found an answer to the problem. According to a long-standing tradition the Metropolitan of Galicia also held, among his honorary titles, that of Bishop of Kamenetz-Podolsk, a town situated within the Russian Empire. This title had never been suppressed officially by an act of canon law. Could it not then be argued that the

Metropolitan of Galicia was authorized, at least temporarily, to take under his guidance Russian Catholic priests of the same rite as his own? Certain Russian Old Believers had acted in a similar way: their bishop gave guidance from abroad to priests who worked in Russia.

On a visit to Rome in 1907, the Metropolitan had put forward his solution to Pope Pius X, and had obtained the Pope's oral consent: *"Utere jure tuo"* (Use your right), the Pontiff had said to him. On his return to Lvov the Metropolitan had therefore, by an act of June 29, 1907, nominated Father Alexis Zerchaninov his vicar-general for the eparchy of Kamenetz-Podolsk. However, the fact that approval had been given only orally and not in writing prevented the Metropolitan from affirming his rights, which were immediately contested. He therefore resolved to return to Rome the following year; this time he had obtained the written approval of Pius X for the powers he had requested.[6]

However, not all difficulties were so easily overcome. Father Zerchaninov had spent four years in confinement for becoming a Catholic, and for the same reason had been separated from his wife and children. He bore a grudge against the Czarist government, and on this score found that he shared the feelings of a fair number of priests of the Latin rite. He came under their influence, and was soon a great admirer of Polish customs, adopting the Western manner of making the sign of the cross—that is, from left to right—and introducing into his chapel forms of devotion modeled on those of Western Catholics, such as benediction of the Blessed Sacrament, the rosary, and so on. The members of his congregation were at first surprised and then annoyed, and most of them left him, placing their confidence in Father Deibner. The latter would have needed very deep clarity of vision and very resistant nerves to keep control of situations which were often complicated and unexpected, and, although he was an extremely pious and zealous man, he did not have these qualities of leadership. In addition, he was married, and his duties as the father of a family occupied a large part of his time.

As for the third priest, Father Eustaphe Sussalev, he was unbelievably peasantlike, and this took away any prestige he might have had in the eyes of the refined St. Petersburgers. For instance, his way of speaking Russian was extremely crude. Miss Ushakov says he had his own way of conjugating the verb "to be able" in Russian. *"My moghim,"* he repeated obstinately in his sermons as well as in his daily speech, instead of *"my mojem."* This would be equivalent to saying in English "we is able" instead of "we are able," and after trying for several months to teach him to speak more grammatically, Miss Ushakov had to admit defeat. Moreover, his convictions as a Catholic were not deep. Just as he had left the Old Believers to become a Catholic, so he soon secretly resolved to leave the Catholics and go over to the Orthodox Church. He went to an Orthodox bishop and suggested that he put himself under his jurisdiction while continuing to live among Catholics, so that he could act as a kind of spy on them. The bishop refused. After this, Father Sussalev disappeared from Catholic circles, and nothing more was heard of him until eight years later, at the time of the Revolution.

"The only person who really gives any effective support to the Catholic community and keeps it going in the right direction is Miss Natalie Ushakov," Leonid wrote in a letter which he sent from St. Petersburg to Metropolitan Andrew at the end of his visit.[7]

CHAPTER SEVEN

Priest and Monk

Miss Ushakov had been right in her appraisal of the situation: this first journey back to Russia convinced Leonid that the time was still not ripe for a genuine understanding between Russia and the Catholic Church. He concluded that it would be useless for him to settle permanently in St. Petersburg and that he had no further reason for delaying his ordination as a priest.

Meanwhile, the movements of Metropolitan Andrew were being viewed with increasing suspicion in Russia. Just as the Austrian government had accused him of supporting Pan-Slavism, so the Russian government tried to represent him as the force behind Ukrainian separatism, a political movement whose purpose was to detach from the Russian Empire those regions in the south where the rural population spoke Ukrainian, the same language as that used in Galicia. To maintain relations with the Metropolitan was very compromising for Russian Catholics. To be ordained by him would give Leonid a still worse and lasting bad name in the

minds of the Czarist police. It was essential to avoid any
misunderstanding on this score, so he decided to leave Russia
and ask to be ordained to the major orders by Mgr. Mirov,
Archbishop of the Bulgarian Catholics, who resided in Constantinople.

In the middle of March 1911, Leonid alighted from the
train on the banks of the Bosphorus, at the foot of the hill
which overhangs Santa Sophia, the basilica of ancient Byzantium, then being used as a mosque by the Turks.

On March 22, 1911, during the Divine Liturgy, he was
ordained subdeacon and deacon * by the Bulgarian archbishop. Sunday, the 26th of the same month, the fifth Sunday
in Lent according to the Julian calendar, was chosen for his
ordination to the priesthood. On that day, before the Divine
Liturgy, Leonid put on the vestments of a deacon for the last
time, and carried out his part as one until after the procession
called "the great entry." Then the usual course of the Eucharistic sacrifice was interrupted; the archbishop took his seat
to the left of the altar, and a priest, holding Leonid by the
arm, led him three times around the holy table. Next the
candidate for ordination knelt with his forehead placed between his hands on the edge of the altar; with his wide Byzantine omophorion (pallium) Archbishop Mirov covered
Leonid's head, and placing his hands above it, proclaimed:
"The grace of God which always heals the sick and supplies
our wants, raises the most pious deacon Leonid to the priesthood. Let us pray for him, that the gift of the Holy Ghost
may descend upon him."

After the other sacramental prayers, the archbishop clothed
him in the vestments of a priest, and with each, following
the custom of the first centuries of the Church, he sang in
Greek *"Axios"*—"He is worthy," and the assistants repeated

* In the Russian Church, these two orders are often conferred on the same
day.

"Axios." In conclusion, the new priest celebrated the rest of the Divine Liturgy with the archbishop by whom he had just been ordained.

When the ceremony was over, Leonid at once sent a post-card to his mother and to Metropolitan Andrew which read: "The Lord has granted my prayers—Leonid priest."

Four months later, that is to say on July 27, 1911, the Third Unionistic Congress opened at Velehrad. This time the number of participants had increased to more than two hundred. As Metropolitan Andrew was sick and unable to attend, Father Leonid, no longer a mere student of theology but a Russian priest and a specialist in problems of the Eastern Church, was chosen as commissary. During the sessions of the Congress he engaged in extremely animated discussions with the Orientalists of the time, in particular with Fathers Palmieri, Jugie and d'Herbigny.

Almost all of those who attended the Congress at Velehrad were Catholics, and, with the exception of the protopriest Alexis Maltzev, chaplain of the Russian Embassy in Berlin, the part played by Orthodox churchmen at these congresses was insignificant. It was clear that these meetings would not become truly productive until the day when they ceased to be Catholic monologues and would become real dialogues with the world of Eastern Christianity separated from Rome. This indeed was the program which had been formulated by the first Congress in 1907: "To open the way for peace and harmony between West and East, to throw light on controversial questions, to correct prejudices, to bring together those who are most hostile to each other, and to restore full friendship . . . so that we may not only gain deeper insight into these problems, but may also exchange views on the best methods to be adopted for action." [1]

Father Feodorov gave a strong lead in this direction. At the end of the third Congress he composed a letter which was signed by Mgr. Epiphanius Shanov, Catholic Bulgarian bishop of Macedonia, and sent to the most notable figures in the Slavonic Churches separated from Rome. In part it read: "We intend to use scientific research to prepare the way for mutual understanding between us. The Congresses of Velehrad are not an exclusively confessional institution (i.e. restricted to Catholics)—but rather a gathering of enlightened men, inspired by a spirit of religion and convinced that disunion is the work of the Devil and that we must destroy it. . . . Only an institution such as ours can permit a vital and constructive exchange of ideas." The letter ended with an invitation to send a delegate to the next Congress which was to take place in August 1914.

Once the Congress was over, Father Feodorov made three successive journeys to St. Petersburg. During his fourth stay in the capital, which lasted from November 1911 to April 1912, he decided to regularize his situation with the government.

Before the Imperial manifesto of October 17, 1905, which granted freedom of worship to the inhabitants of the Empire, it had been forbidden in Russia to go over from Orthodoxy to any other religion. After the promulgation of the manifesto this was permitted, provided application be first made to the chief of police, and that the convert then undergo what was known as an *uveshchanye*, or interrogation and exhortation, by an Orthodox doctor of theology.

Father Leonid had been a Catholic for ten years, but his identity papers and his passport still identified him as an Orthodox, since he had not complied with the required formalities. He therefore handed in his request at the police headquarters. "I was sent to Archpriest George Poliansky, rector of the Church of Our Lady, in the Pesky quarter" [of St. Petersburg], he writes. "He was a good and venerable old man who greeted me kindly and courteously. First he asked me my surname, my 'patronymic' and my first name, as well as the other usual information, and then proceeded to the monition.

"He looked at me enquiringly, but in a friendly way nonetheless. 'I would very much like to know,' he said, 'how you became convinced of the truth of the Roman Catholic Church?' "

"I was in an awkward situation," Father Leonid says. "Had my questioner been younger, I should not have cared what I said, but I saw before me a good and venerable old man, who was clearly embarrassed by the part which he was obliged to play.

" 'What can I say, Father? I reached my conviction through a rather complex psychological process. In general terms, I might say that it was through study. I have read the Fathers of the Church, the Acts of the Councils and other ancient ecclesiastical documents, and I have come to see that the truth is on the side of the Catholics.'

" 'Ah! So you are deeply convinced then?'

" 'Obviously.'

" 'Yes, of course.'

"An awkward silence followed. Both of us were afraid of making a wrong move, and we did not know how to get out of this unfortunate situation. Finally, to break the silence, I said to him: 'Listen, Father, this is a simple formality. A long time ago, Minister Sazonov, when he was Russian representative in the Vatican, gave me permission to stay abroad longer than the time stated on my passport. This permission was granted me as a pupil of the College 'De Propaganda Fide,' that is to say, as a Catholic. I have already been a Catholic for nine years, and a priest for nearly a year.'

" 'Yes, I understand; clearly this is a simple formality. But what can we do? It is demanded of us!'

"A further silence followed, and then the good priest said to me, smiling: 'Yes, De Propaganda Fide . . .'

" 'It is a most interesting establishment, Father: Japanese, Chinese, Americans and many other races go there.'

" 'Yes, indeed, that is very interesting.'

"There was another silence and then I said: 'Father, don't keep me by formalities, I beg of you; I want to go abroad as soon as possible.'

" 'Don't worry,' he replied, giving me a friendly handshake, 'I am going to pass on the documents to the authorities at once. Good-by, and my best wishes!' "

The monition had lasted barely ten minutes, and Father Leonid's passport was duly altered.[2]

In St. Petersburg, a feeling of pessimism was spreading among the Russian Catholics. The opposition of the Polish clergy, the eccentricities of Father Zerchaninov and his misunderstandings with Father Deibner, as well as the known hostility of the government, had awakened a certain mood of discouragement among them. In an attempt to overcome this, Father Leonid arranged to stay with the Catholics of the capital over Easter, 1912. He tells us that he himself wiped away the dust and the cobwebs which had gathered in the chapel, bought brooms, new sacred vessels and altar cloths, and on Easter night celebrated matins and the Liturgy with Fathers Zerchaninov and Deibner. Seventy people were present at the service.

The police were watching, and an officer came and asked Father Alexis why this young priest was celebrating the service with him.

"He's a Catholic priest," Father Alexis answered. "We cannot forbid him to hold services with us." And the policeman went away without further questions. But Father Leonid clearly perceived that he could not remain in St. Petersburg without creating further difficulties for the little community of Russian Catholics.

A few days later, he again crossed the frontier into Austria-Hungary.

Earlier, while Leonid was studying as a young man at the Ecclesiastical Academy, the wish to practice a more rigorous and disciplined form of the monastic life had excited his first interest in the Catholic Church, and had then drawn him toward it. During his training for the priesthood this desire had grown stronger; he was greatly attracted to the life of prayer and work led by the Jesuits of Anagni, the Benedictines of the Greek College in Rome, and the Camaldolese Fathers who lived as hermits in the hillsides of Central Italy. He now saw this vocation as his own way of life and as a preparation for his apostolate in Russia.

"My greatest wish," he confided one day to a friend, "is to work in St. Petersburg with two or three Russian monks. What a spiritual harvest we could gather there!" [3]

In Lvov and Galicia, the Basilian Fathers followed the religious life in the Byzantine rite, but they had been reformed by the Jesuits at the request of Pope Leo XIII, and had adopted a Western approach to monastic life, dividing their time between action and contemplation. For those who were eager for a more enclosed life, Metropolitan Andrew, though himself a Basilian, had created a monastic foundation in the spirit of the former Byzantine monastery of Studion in Constantinople. The first *lavra* of the Studite monks was opened by him in the Carpathians, at Sknilov. Their life, shared between the celebration of the complete Byzantine divine office and work in the fields, in many ways resembled that of the Trappists in the Western Church. This first *lavra* grew to such an extent that a second foundation was undertaken at Kamenitza, in Bosnia, whose inhabitants were Ukrainian. Feeling attracted to this young monastery, Father Leonid asked to be admitted, and entered there on May 20, 1912.

In accordance with Russian monastic custom, the religious name he took began with the same letter as his baptismal one; he chose to be called Father Leontii, in honor of the martyr of that name. From the first he wanted as complete a break with the world as possible within the bounds of charity, and he wrote to Metropolitan Andrew that only letters from his mother were to be forwarded to him.

Each night he got up to sing the offices and matins, and during the day returned for long hours to celebrate the Holy Liturgy and other monastic prayers. The monastery was really poor, and the monks had to work hard to survive. From eight in the morning until midday, Father Leontii hammered nails, sawed and planed wood in the joiner's workshop, and during the afternoon worked in the vineyards which were the chief source of the monastery's income. In addition to this, there was work to be done on the farm. Sixteen months after his entry, this man, who had at one time been the guest of Mr. Sazonov and of the Roman Cardinals, could write: "We have just bought two piglets, and the job of fattening them has been given to me. This is an occupation that suits me admirably. I think of myself in all seriousness as the prodigal son who wasted his substance in riotous living and has to herd swine far away from his Father's house. When will I be able to say in true sincerity, 'Father, I have sinned against heaven and in Thy sight?' "

"I can easily bear the harsh discipline of our life," he wrote to Metropolitan Andrew, "due to my robust health and to my capacity to adapt myself. Of course, at the beginning I suffered from the lack of food, on top of heavy manual work. At times I even rebelled against it. There is only one terrible enemy, however, which I have so far been unable to overcome, and that is sleep. When I feel drowsy in church, I am forced to recognize the miserable impotence of my will . . .

". . . I feel that for the first time I am beginning to live for myself, to live as I have wished to for a long time. The sweetest thing for me is to feel my isolation from the world and my total forgetfulness of all its vanities and of all its petty concerns." [4]

After a retreat, he noted: "Since I joined the Catholic Church, that is to say, for the past ten years, I have worked night and day for it, and yet I feel that I have passed my whole life in idleness. I have left unheeded so many evident inspirations of the grace of God. My lack of recollection, despite the splendid education I received from the Jesuits of Anagni, left my will soft and feeble, fearful of taking any positive step. Everything concerning my future life and activity was shrouded in an immense *dubium,* a hesitation, and my mind amused itself with sophistries, trying to escape from a clear call to the ascetic life. My heart bleeds now at the eternal loss of my youthful ardor and enthusiasm. I remember what one of my Jesuit confessors once said to me: '*Vous avez été trop prudent dans toutes vos délibérations, et à cause de cela vous pouvez perdre la grâce de Dieu.*' * This is a paradox, but in my case it is true. We must have more trust in Providence which will guide us and spread its favors in our path, if we know how to turn to it with faith and with childlike simplicity.

"Another result of my retreat is a firm resolution to begin, with God's help, to lead an angelic supernatural life, and to start by keeping silence and recollection. The very last day of the retreat was my thirty-third birthday, and with tears in my eyes I asked God to help me to become an accomplished monk at this age when He Himself finished the work of our Redemption . . ." [5]

Further on he admits: "My retreat did not pass without temptation. I had a strong desire to read theology or to write

* "You have been too prudent in all your deliberations, and because of this you risk losing the grace of God." This phrase was written in French while the rest of the letter was in Russian.

down some notes on the liturgy. I was also eager to know how
the war with the Turks was progressing. [This was at the time
of the War in the Balkans.] My fanatical hatred of the Turks
gives me no rest. I sucked it with my mother's milk. Night
and day I dreamed only of that happy moment when the
Cross would once again shine from the dome of Aghia Sophia.
In my daydreams I even imagined myself as one of the Greek
sharpshooters.' "

In his solitary meditation the reconciliation of Russia with
the Roman Catholic Church appeared to him as it really was:
a task apparently far beyond human capabilities. He was
sometimes tempted to abandon his work and cease to dream
of this reconciliation. How could mutual ignorance and the
violent hostility of certain people be overcome? How could
one dispel prejudices on both sides which were so deeply
rooted, although often founded on so little? Above all, how
was one to arouse the indifferent and awake the interest of the
masses in this vitally important question?

"I am no longer successful in intellectual work," he told
himself, "and manual work is going magnificently. A voice
sometimes tells me: 'Stay calm, pray, and don't concern yourself with anything beyond that.' Is not a fear of apostolic
work hidden beneath these feelings? Apostolic work brings
with it so many worries, so much responsibility, reflection
and action in every quarter. Here, on the other hand, there
is perfect calm. All that is left are the tranquilizing liturgical
offices, the standing stations, and the processions during
which, carried away by the liturgical chanting, men can
forget everything in the world and be transported to the
paradise of spiritual delight. This is but a step from spiritual
lethargy and the seduction of quietism, which is the most
terrible thing that can attack a monk. . . ." [6]

He discovered another tendency in himself: hardness of
heart toward his neighbors. And indeed they did not hesitate

to point it out to him. The honest monks he met at Kamenitza were rough countrymen and bore no resemblance to his friends in St. Petersburg or Rome. "Above all, I find it very hard to get used to my new companions," he admitted. "Among our monks here we lack intelligent and cultured men, and their outlook is not the same as mine; I must get beneath their skins to understand them and for them to understand me. Sometimes I have to listen to the most unlikely stories about the saints and their fantastic miracles. I have to bite my lips to prevent myself from bursting into laughter. At times I really find myself regretting their religious ignorance and their lack of culture."

However, he managed to control his impatience and to cease from showing it. One of his companions later said of him: "Father Leontii lived in so saintly a manner that he never said an unkind word to anyone. His way of talking was very gentle, and he always kept a perfectly even temper." [7]

During the three hundred years that they have been joined to the Latin Church, Greek Catholics have altered a good number of their former liturgical traditions and have adopted Latin devotional practices. In St. Petersburg, Father Alexis Zerchaninov, under the influence of the Polish clergy, had aroused discontent among his congregation by doing this very thing. This question was one of prime importance at the monastery of Kamenitza, for the monks wanted to follow the Byzantine liturgical tradition in all its purity, yet at the same time they could not forget their ties with the Latin Church. The problem was one which could be solved only by very delicate handling: Why should the rite be kept in absolute fixity? Surely everything which is human must progress, thus evolving and adopting itself to the needs of the time?

In some of his writings of the period, Father Leontii again took up ideas which he had previously put forward at the Congresses of Velehrad. First he insisted on one fundamental point: that the conception of rite is not the same in the Western Church and in the Eastern Church. In the minds of many Roman Catholics, Eastern Christians are characterized by the fact that they celebrate their services in a language other than Latin, that the prayers and the gestures of the priest are different, that their diocesan clergy is married, and that they wear beards and give Communion under two species. For such Catholics the differences are summarized by these details.

In actual fact, the difference is chiefly concerned with the union which exists in the East between dogma and the liturgy. "The Eastern Christian," wrote Father Feodorov, "only knows extremes; he is not conscious of the Western *distinguo;* he understands only *affirmo* and *nego*. Hence his inability to distinguish between faith and rite. If one tries to explain to him the distinction between rite and faith by comparing it to that between a means and an end, or between an accessory and the essential, he will exclude the rite completely from his religious practices and confine himself strictly to prayer and sermons. This is how the Russian sects acted, and also the Muslims or the Buddhists of Burma, Siam and Ceylon." [8]

In a letter of guidance, Metropolitan Andrew had felt that he ought to put him on his guard against a kind of Eastern chauvinism which might blind him to the spiritual value of the West. "I am very glad," Father Leontii answered, "that you have raised this question of the 'universalist spirit,' and that you put me on my guard against Eastern ritual chauvinism. I can now answer you in greater detail.

"Where do you think I would go if it chanced that my experience with the Studites failed to satisfy me? There is no doubt that I would go over to the Latin rite. I have already chosen the Order of the Sylvestrines for myself as the last stage in my efforts to reach perfection. It would need something very serious to turn me away from this decision. Now say that

you are afraid that I will fall into Eastern chauvinism and
lack Catholic spirit. You would find it hard, I think, to discover another Eastern Catholic who considers the question
of rite as calmly as I do. But wherever I happen to be, in an
Eastern rite or in a Latin rite, I will be faithful to it in the
marrow of my bones, and I will never let myself become a
Latin-Eastern bastard. *Sentire cum Ecclesia.* It is a great principle, and I have adopted it to the very depth of my being,
and it is precisely because of this principle that I do not wish
to lead any other life than that which the Holy Church pre-
scribes for me.

"As an example of my Eastern fanaticism, people claim that
I do not venerate the Western saints. If this were true, I
would not pray, as I do daily, to St. Thomas Aquinas and St.
Francis de Sales; and I would not observe the feast of St.
Ignatius Loyola on July 31 every year in so special a way. But
is it not natural that every Church should venerate especially
its own saints—those who represent its own particular spirit?
Is this not precisely what is done by the religious Orders? In
fact, the East, as far as the veneration of saints is concerned,
has kept a more universal spirit than the West, and one which
is also more true to the tradition of the first centuries of
Christianity. The Jesuits of Anagni exalted their St. Aloysius
Gonzaga to the third heaven, but they altogether disregarded
St. John the Baptist, although he is 'the greatest man born
of woman.' " [9]

However, his attachment to Eastern traditions did not blind
the young Studite hieromonk to those ways in which the West
is in advance of the East, in the harmonious rational synthesis
it has achieved between dogma and moral laws, and in the
way in which it stimulates a desire of strictly conforming
conduct to faith. He wrote that as soon as he had time he
would compose in Russian a manual for performing the
Spiritual Exercises of St. Ignatius.

"I have been through its schools," the letter ends, "and I know perfectly well the progress made by the Latin branch of the Church in the field of the development of Christian thought: theology, philosophy, the practice of confession, the cult of the holy Eucharist, the development of the religious Orders, the veneration of the Sacred Heart, and the study of dogma. In these fields we are their humble disciples, and we borrow from them all that we need. But at the same time we recognize the failings of our great sister [the Latin Church], which are the result of its long separation from the holy and mystical East: for example, a decrease in asceticism, and also utilitarianism, narrowness of outlook, and a lack of aesthetic sense in the liturgy or of vivacity and simplicity in faith."

A friend with whom he had been speaking told him that the Jesuits do not like Eastern liturgies. Father Leontii answered: "They have no special dislike for the Eastern liturgies as such; it would be more correct to say that they simply dislike every liturgy. . . . They have lost sight of their symbolic content. They tend to encourage forms of ceremony which, although for a time may impress the imagination, are basically superficial and sentimental and, being less rich in symbolic meaning, do not nourish the piety of the faithful in as deep and stable a manner as the ceremonies of the Greco-Russian Church."

The good Studite monks of Kamenitza kept most of the latinizations (or Latin usages) in their rubrics which were introduced by the Greco-Catholics into the Byzantine rite during their three centuries of union with Rome: rectangular altars, for instance, flowers in the sanctuary, low Masses and so on. Father Leontii considered it a duty not to encourage them, and therefore he asked to celebrate the Divine Liturgy alone every day in the sacristy where he could observe the rubrics without tolerating any changes.

The notes he sent at that time to Metropolitan Andrew,

who was his spiritual guide, show that these considerations of the liturgy and Eastern spirituality did not distract his attention from the essentials of his monastic life: the fight for humility, purity of intention and sincere love of God. "Last year," he writes, "after Easter I made my first step in the monastic life. I gave up eating meat, I attended all the services, I slept on a wooden couch. Everything seemed to me extraordinarily easy; even heavy work was a diversion for me. And instead of thanking the Lord for making the monastic exercises easy for me, I focused my attention on the capacity of my nature which so easily overcame all obstacles . . . and then the Lord made me feel my nothingness. . . . Often the Superman who overcomes great moral obstacles falls to small temptations. Vanity shows itself sometimes under the most tragic and ridiculous forms. May I give you an example? As soon as I entered the monastery, I immediately began to wear a leather belt and to follow the monastic rules. This, of course, could not escape notice; everybody thought that I had really made up my mind to become a monk. Then I learned that some were saying of me that . . . 'I was not a stupid fellow' and that . . . 'I knew how to secure a mitre for myself'! The blood rushed to my head: 'How can one think of me that I am aspiring—as so many others do—for glory and honor?' I paced my room like a wild animal in its cage; I threw away my paltry belt and did not put it on for two days . . . and then I became aware of the weakness of my soul. While I thought I was really independent of what other people thought of me, I had been completely dependent on them . . . and from what kind of people? On a cook and a servant who have no control of their tongues. A really humble man would have accepted such a humiliation and would have thanked God . . . how that incident would have untied the strings of his inner vanity, how grateful to the Lord the humble man would have been. . . .

"The old desire of reaching spiritual summits remains in me, but it has not assumed a purely Christian nature. I experience, obviously, a great attraction to the monastic life, but then the question rises: Will I succeed in changing my nature, in throwing away my old skin? Will I ever succeed in getting rid of my Buddhist Stoicism and of my selfishness?"

CHAPTER EIGHT

Trouble in St. Petersburg

WHILE the hieromonk Leontii was engaged in solitary prayer and meditation and in work with the hammer, the pitchfork, and sometimes also with the pen, Natalie Ushakov in St. Petersburg bravely continued her struggle on three fronts. She had to combat the increasing hostility of the Polish clergy toward the Russian parish and the growing eccentricities of Father Alexis; above all she struggled with the representatives of the government to obtain official recognition of the Russian parish, without which the fate of the enterprise would always hang in the balance.

After applying many times, she managed to get an interview, on January 3, 1912, with Mr. Makarov, the Minister of the Interior. Again she repeated her request that the community be granted the same rights as those enjoyed by foreigners in Russia—that is to say, the right to have its own church, its own priests and its sermon in Russian.

Mr. Makarov: "Zerchaninov will be given legal recognition. But it is impossible to do that in the case of Deibner, who has hidden the fact that he is a priest."

Miss Ushakov: "He did not hide it when he was questioned. It is true that he did not come and declare it, but there is a difference. At that time there was no church; the manifesto of religious toleration had not then been published, and we did not enjoy our present theoretical liberty. Why should he go and declare that he was a priest? But now that he has regularized his situation, we wish to have him as a priest."

Mr. Makarov: "And why do you not go to the French church?"

Miss Ushakov: "Because we do not belong there; we want our own church!"

At this point, the minister rose and stood in silence for quite a long time. Miss Ushakov also rose, and went on with what she had been saying:

"It is understandable that the Poles should persecute us and denounce us; we exist for the simple reason that we want to prevent our brothers, the Russian Catholics, from joining them. But why does the government persecute us when we are its faithful subjects, when we do not engage in politics and when we want only one thing—to keep the Russians for Russia and to worship God in our own way, as we have been accustomed to do. . . ."

Mr. Makarov: "But what are you saying? This is Unia!" [The name "Unia," which carried overtones of aversion and contempt, was given by certain Eastern Orthodox churchmen to the Union of Brest-Litovsk of 1596, by which certain eparchies, or dioceses, of Byzantine rite then situated on the borders of Poland and Russia announced their union with Rome.]

Miss Ushakov: "I don't know what it is called in Russia. Everywhere else in the world it is known as Catholicism of the Eastern rite. In the name of our group, I have come to ask for your support. We do not live behind locked doors;

why not come and watch us? We are not afraid of that. We simply demand that we should be allowed our rights."

Mr. Makarov: "I know that, and I will give the matter careful consideration."

The minister took leave of his visitor and she retired. Three months later, in March, she received a curt official letter telling her that no permission could yet be granted, and that an enquiry had first to be made into the "correct political attitudes of the parishioners." [1]

However, Miss Ushakov was less upset by this than by the attitude of the newly appointed Latin Ordinary of Mohiliov, Archbishop Kliuchinsky, in whose diocese the Catholics of St. Petersburg lived. Partly, it was thought, through personal dislike and partly through extreme fear of the government, he was always finding new pretexts to hinder the movements of the Russian Catholics and to delay as long as possible the execution of orders which he received from Rome regarding them.

The problem of purity of rite was still the subject of bitter and long drawn-out controversies. With the wholehearted approval of Archbishop Kliuchinsky, Father Zerchaninov defended the latinisms that he had introduced into the Byzantine ceremonies. To this certain Russian Catholics replied that as their final aim was the union of the Russian and the Roman Churches, they must demonstrate not only in words but in facts and actions that in the event of union the Russian Church would not have to change any of its liturgical traditions. Father Deibner was upset by these conflicts and was left confused and undecided.

At last the Assumptionist Fathers in St. Petersburg persuaded Rome to enter the discussion. Cardinal Merry del Val, at that time Papal Secretary of State, wrote to Archbishop Kliuchinsky to say that Catholic priests of Byzantine rite should perform the offices in exactly the same way as the priests of the Russian Synodal Church, neither removing, adding nor changing anything. *Nec plus, nec minus, nec aliter,* he wrote in Latin. These words were to become a concise formula which was often to be referred to as a clear guide for the solution of future problems. The Cardinal Secretary of State went on to say that the Roman clergy, including the Archbishop of Mohiliov, should not intervene in liturgical questions concerning the Russian Catholics.[2]

Since Miss Ushakov knew from other sources that the Pope supported her, she went forward. As a Catholic of Byzantine rite, she was not under the jurisdiction of the Archbishop of Mohiliov, so she decided to take no notice of his ill-will toward them. To the north of St. Petersburg, in the part of the city called Petersburgskaya Storona, at No. 42 Barmalayeva Ulitsa (Street), she rented a fairly large apartment and organized a new chapel where Father Deibner alone would celebrate the Holy Liturgy in the full purity of the Byzantine rite. The chapel was solemnly consecrated on September 30, 1912, in the presence of a large congregation and with the singing of an excellent choir, that essential element of ceremonies in the Russian rite.

Miss Ushakov was filled with happiness. The same day she wrote to her friend Princess Marie Volkonsky, then in Rome: "If only you could see how pretty our chapel is! The iconostasis is white with some gilding, but light and without glitter. The Liturgy was sung after the chapel had been blessed. I could only thank God for His kindness to us during this year. I forgot everything, even the mean actions of Father Alexis toward us. Of course, he did not come to the ceremony, and he will not come to see us. On the contrary, he sent a deputation to Mgr. Kliuchinsky to ask him not to give permission for the chapel to be transferred, but it was already too late. Mgr. Kliuchinsky behaves in an odd way toward Father Deibner, and he took the side of Father Zerchaninov. 'It is no use for you to move to another place,' he told him, 'I will not go and see you, and you can expect no financial help from me. In any case, it is clear that we do not understand each other.' " [3]

Miss Ushakov had the support of the French religious living in St. Petersburg, especially of the Dominican Father Lagrange and of the Assumptionist Father Beaurain. Eventually the Latin bishop also became more favorable. At the end of the year, Natalie Ushakov wrote to her friend: "No doubt Mgr. Kliuchinsky has had a letter from Cardinal Merry del Val, for his attitude towards Father Deibner has altogether changed. For the first time he has behaved toward him in a friendly manner." [4]

The activity of the parish was not confined to the liturgical services. A group was organized to help the poor, and in January 1913 the first issue of a Russian Catholic monthly was printed with the title *Slovo Istini*—The Word of Truth.

Unfortunately, the parish was not to be left to live in peace for more than three months. Father Deibner did something without the full consent of his parishioners which could have been misunderstood, and which laid him open to criticism. At the entrance to the building in which his chapel was situated, he put a notice reading "Catholic Orthodox Church." In addition to their precise etymological meaning, the words "Catholic" and "Orthodox" have acquired very definite historical ones. Of course Father Deibner could call his church "Orthodox," since to his mind the only real truth was preached in it, but for by far the greater numbers of the passers-by, the word "Orthodox" implied the Russian national Church not united with Rome. The priest was weakening his own good cause by not adopting a clear and irreproachable

position in this matter, and his devoted friends, among them
Princess Marie Volkonsky, had tried in vain to persuade him
of this.

On Sunday, February 10, 1913 (according to the Julian
calendar), some minutes before he began the Holy Liturgy,
Father Deibner was incensing the sanctuary and the altar,
when suddenly Mgr. Nicandre, Orthodox bishop of Narva
and coadjutor of the Metropolitan of St. Petersburg, burst
into the chapel. He went directly into the sanctuary, behind
the iconostasis, and the congregation in the chapel heard
voices raised in argument. Father Deibner asked the visitor
not to interrupt the service which was about to begin, but the
bishop replied: "Who are you? Who ordained you?"

Bishop Nicandre then left the sanctuary, made the sign
of the cross, and turning to the congregation, proclaimed:

"I came into this church in the belief that it was Orthodox;
I went as far as the sanctuary, and there everything is Catholic. Orthodox churchmen, you are being deceived! This is
a Roman Catholic church which does not have the authorization of the government. Where are the police? Proceedings
must be instituted against you. Anathema! If you do not leave
this place, you will be cursed! Anathema!"

At this moment Father Deibner, wearing his vestments,
came out from behind the iconostasis and in his turn addressed the congregation:

"No doubt His Lordship speaks in ignorance of the facts:
this church has been authorized by the ecclesiastical and civil
authorities. My brothers, fear nothing, stay firm in your faith,
and the Lord will not desert you. Let us pray together for
our brothers in the Orthodox Church who have not yet received the fullness of faith which has been granted to us by
the mercy of God. Let us forgive our enemies that the Lord
may forgive us in our turn, and let us pray for them."

While Father Deibner was speaking, Bishop Nicandre left

the chapel. A layman in the congregation went up to Father Deibner and said: "He is right, Father: this is deceit. I am going." He was the only one to leave. While the bishop was in the chapel, three men had been waiting for him on the staircase.

The next day, the papers were filled with news of this happening. *Novoye Vremya,* the most important daily, carried the headline, "Jesuits in St. Petersburg!" and the other papers of the capital gave dramatic accounts of the event. The police were impressed by this outcry, and sealed up the two chapels in Barmalayeva Street and in Polozovaya Street.

Miss Ushakov went directly to protest to Mr. Menkin, head of the Department of Foreign Religions. She was told that "services had not been authorized in that form," and that it had been thought that the community was conducting the Latin Mass in Russian.

"What!" Natalie Ushakov replied indignantly, "for the last four years, we have not stopped writing and making appeals in order that Russians who believe in conscience that they should go over to Catholicism might be permitted to keep the rite to which they are accustomed. We insist that we want to preserve them from latinization or from Polonization, and now you tell us that no one knew in what form our services were conducted!"

Natalie Ushakov continued to do all she could to have the seals removed. Mr. Nicholas Lvov promised to raise the question in the Duma. "I am doing all that I can," Miss Ushakov wrote to Princess Marie Volkonsky at this time. "But I am without hope. Pray for me, so that I do not complain or become wicked and submit myself. I was so happy about everything, and then suddenly this has to happen!" [5]

At the end of March, a new disappointment was in store for the community of Catholic Russians. Mr. Nicholas Lvov, the parliamentary representative, said that he could not bring

the matter before the Duma since the Catholic Ordinary,
Archbishop Kliuchinsky, had not protested the closing of the
chapels. The latter's silence in the matter implied dis-
approval of Father Deibner, and it would be impossible for
the Duma to support a priest who seemed to be under censure
by his bishop.[6]

The foreign press reported the incident and of course Pope
Pius X was informed. The Roman Pontiff could not intervene with the Czarist government, but he sent Father Deibner
a letter of approval and encouragement which gave very great
comfort to the group.

At the time this news reached Kamenitza, the hieromonk
Leontii was considering a voyage to the East, and especially
to Mount Athos, hoping to gain inspiration from the best
traditions of the Eastern monasteries which he planned to
visit. However, he now realized that it was his duty to alter
his plans. At the end of the year, setting aside his personal
wishes, he arrived unexpectedly in St. Petersburg.

His presence there at once put new heart into the Catholic
community. A short time after his arrival, he assembled its
most active members in Father Deibner's house; they all
came, including Father Alexis Zerchaninov, who had never
before visited Father Deibner at his home. Father Leontii—
now once again Father Leonid, since this was the only name
by which he was known to the faithful in St. Petersburg—
praised them for their courage and begged them to remain
united, since this was the only way in which they could
achieve their ends. So moved were his hearers that even
Father Alexis publicly expressed regret at his former opposition, and embraced the speaker three times. When they left
they were imbued with new strength, almost with enthusiasm, and had determined to meet again each Friday.

In an account written during this trip, Father Leonid states
that the parish at this time numbered forty-three very militant

Catholics, including, however, nine children, to whom could be added at least seven hundred others who lived too far away from the chapel to be able to attend its services regularly.

The chapel itself had remained intact, and the faithful confidently waited for better days when they could reopen it. At the time of its closing the police had sealed up the outer door, but had overlooked an inner door through which it could still be entered. Father Leonid did not hesitate to take advantage of this omission, and again quietly began to hold services there. The windows on the street were curtained, and during Holy Week, 1914, surrounded by the most fervent and reliable of the parishioners, he celebrated the offices of Good Friday, Holy Saturday and of Easter night.

But the police were on the alert. In early April, Father Feodorov received an anonymous letter in which the writer said that she had learned from friends of his unexpected arrival in St. Petersburg. She described her spiritual struggles and the danger of sin which threatened her. She said that she could not come to see him, but begged him to grant her an interview, ending her letter: "Do not forsake me; your arrival is my salvation. I beg you to be at the corner of Nevsky Prospect and St. Catherine's Square, in front of the jeweler's shop, at 3 o'clock next Tuesday." She signed herself "Maria D." Father Leonid questioned some of his friends, but none of them could tell him anything about this person, so he ignored the letter.

The block in which the Catholic chapel was situated faced on two streets, Barmalayeva Street and Pushkarskaya Street. The following day, as Father Leonid was about to leave the house to go into town, he noticed that there were two men at each exit watching, and one of them followed him. He managed to throw him off, but the next day he saw the same four men before the house where he was staying. Again he managed to elude them, but he decided to leave St. Petersburg for Moscow without further delay. A few days later, the woman who had sheltered him was called to see the chief of police and severely reprimanded for having had a secretary of Metropolitan Sheptitzky in her house.

Father Leonid's stay in the capital had three very tangible results. He had revived the hopes of the Catholic parish; he had composed a new petition for the opening of a chapel to be presented to the government; and finally he had saved the magazine *Slovo Istini* from collapse. He wrote some articles for it himself, found eighteen contributors for it, and increased the number of its subscribers to more than three hundred.

In Moscow, he found a group of Russian Catholics led by Mr. and Mrs. Abrikosov, whose members were very pious, but they had no priest and were more concerned with the inner life than with making converts. "The chief aim of the Russian Catholic community here is to sanctify its present members," [7] he wrote after this visit. From Moscow he continued his journey through Nizhni-Novgorod, Saratov and Riazan, and finally left Russia across the frontier into Rumania.

Meanwhile, throughout Europe, men were fearing more and more the threat of approaching war. The great nations were sharpening their swords.

CHAPTER NINE

War—Exile in Siberia

"War is inevitable," Father Leonid wrote to Metropolitan Andrew at the end of the account of his journey to Russia.

He was not mistaken. A few days later, on June 29, 1914, newspapers throughout the world headlined the assassination of Archduke Francis Ferdinand, heir to the Austria-Hungarian throne. In the month that followed diplomatic tension increased daily between Austria and Serbia, as also between their respective allies, Germany and Russia.

On July 28, Austria-Hungary declared war on Serbia, and on August 1, the German Ambassador handed his country's declaration of war to the Czar's Minister for Foreign Affairs. This minister was none other than Mr. Sazonov, the former diplomat Leonid had met in Rome. Six days later, Austria-Hungary followed Germany, and, with the exception of a few privileged nations, the whole world entered on a bitter struggle that was to last four years and to alter the face of the Old World. By declaring war on each other, the empires of Germany, Austria-Hungary and Russia had signed their own death warrants.

When war broke out, Father Leonid was in Constantinople, preparing, it seems, for his long intended journey to Mount Athos. He had no time to lose, for as a Russian subject in Turkey, which was then the ally of Germany and Austria, he might be arrested as a spy, and the least that could happen to him would be internment for the duration of the war. At once he took a boat for Odessa; as it turned out this was the last civilian boat for almost four years to leave the Bosphorus for Russia. Two or three days later, Father Leonid was in St. Petersburg, which had just been renamed Petrograd by decree of the Czar.

There he met with two painful surprises: first, he found his mother, Lyubov Dimitryevna, confined to bed, stricken with a paralysis from which she could not be expected to recover. And then, a fortnight after his arrival, the police came to tell him that he was to be deported to Tobolsk in Siberia; he had to leave the capital at once, and the duration of his exile was not specified.

In the time of the Czars, those deported to Siberia generally made the long journey freely—that is to say, without guards—but at their own expense. Only those deportees who were completely penniless had to travel in convoys by stages, and under frightful conditions. It seems that Father Leonid was allowed to make the journey alone, but as soon as he arrived in Tobolsk, he had to go to be registered at the local police headquarters, and from then on to report there at regular intervals, at least once a month.

Tobolsk at this time had a population of about 30,000, and was the administrative center of a huge province, situated in very picturesque surroundings, about 100 miles from the frontier with Europe. The town's economy centered on the Irtych, a wide river which runs through it, and most of its inhabitants lived as fishermen. The rest were tradesmen, artisans, civil servants and above all soldiers. There was a cathedral and about twenty other Orthodox churches, a seminary, a monastery for men, a Polish Catholic church, and finally a Lutheran temple. Father Leonid found it a fairly comfortable place of exile. He rented a room in town and, to earn his living, obtained employment as a clerk in the local government services. In his free time he went down to see the fishermen on the Irtych. These simple men reminded him of the monks of Kamenitza, and he made friends with them, lending them a hand whenever he could.

He also met the teachers at the local Orthodox seminary, and soon became familiar with the books in their library. In this distant part of Siberia, he found ancient works of theology written in Latin at the time when the Orthodox theologians of Kiev, encouraged by their Metropolitan, Peter Mohila, had been inspired by Catholic methods to resist the religious propaganda of the Poles.

Tobolsk was also the home of three or four hundred Catholics, but they were all of Polish origin, and violently opposed to everything Russian. Had Father Leonid tried to conduct services in their church they would have accused him of "Russifying" it; so he was obliged to celebrate the Divine Liturgy in his private apartment.

Parcels reached him regularly from Petrograd, together with news of the war and of the activities of the Russian Catholics there. He had not been long in Siberia when he learned of the swift advance of Russian troops into Galicia, of the capture of Lvov and the assimilation of the province into the Russian Empire.

Following the occupation of Lvov by the Czarist troops, Metropolitan Sheptitzky was confined to his archiepiscopal palace, and three days later, on September 18, 1914, he was sent to Kiev and from there to Kursk, where he was held for a year. Finally the police bundled him into a third class railway carriage, and took him to Vladimir and finally to Suzdal, where he was shut up in the prison-monastery for immoral priests. This was the same prison in which Father Zerchaninov had been incarcerated fifteen years earlier as punishment for becoming a Catholic.

People in Russia were shocked by the brutal way in which the government treated a metropolitan archbishop. Deputy Kerensky took up his cause in the Duma, and the writer Korolenko in the press. The government was accused of following a one-sided, anti-Catholic policy in Galicia which had aroused the hostility of the population and was therefore injurious to the real interests of Russia. These attacks produced the desired result, and in early September 1916, Leonid learned that the Metropolitan had been sent to Yaroslav, the city in which his family had originated.

Although the Catholic community of Petrograd was unmolested, it was still divided. Father Zerchaninov continued to conduct services in one of the side chapels of the Polish Church of St. Catherine; Father Deibner prayed regularly with a small group of faithful parishioners in the chapel in Barmalayeva Street, still entered by the side door which the police had neglected to seal up; and a third Russian priest, Father Gleb Verkovsky, who had been trained in Belgium and ordained in Bulgaria, celebrated the Liturgy in the Latin Church of the Knights of Malta. Meanwhile everyone watched and waited for news from the front.

Early in the winter of 1914 the Catholic community in Petrograd was caused anxiety by a letter from Tobolsk in which Father Leonid told of an illness which had confined him to bed and which might prove to be of long duration. Accustomed to the temperate weather of southern Europe, the young priest had felt the effects of the harsh Siberian climate; furthermore, he had been so unwise as to bathe in the icy waters of the Irtych, and was now suffering from a severe attack of rheumatic fever.

As Madame Feodorov, his mother, was an old woman and also ill, there was no question of her being able to go to care for her son. A volunteer came forward to take her place; this was an elderly Catholic widow, the mother of two children, Madame Kapitolina Ivanova Podlivakhin. The members of the Catholic community all contributed to pay for her journey, and under her care Father Leonid was able to recover the use of his limbs sooner than the doctors had anticipated.

With the passing of the years 1915 and 1916, anyone with insight into the affairs of Russia realized that a feeling of weariness and dissatisfaction was fast growing in the army and among the people. The national economy had been disrupted by the war, and essential commodities were either completely unobtainable or else could only be bought at prices far beyond the reach of the masses. With the constant increase in their sufferings, the ordinary people began to lose patience.

At the front many soldiers had been killed through lack of weapons or because their equipment was insufficient or unsuitable. The morale of the army fell steadily. The Duma complained bitterly, but in vain, against the policy of the government, while the intellectuals and many members of the aristocracy were exasperated by the presence at the imperial court of the Siberian peasant Rasputin and his influence on the Empress.

As early as 1914, at the time of his last journey to Russia, Father Leonid had written: "Gradually the country is preparing for revolution." This time it was inevitable, despite the deep attachment of the Russian people to their ancient traditions. On February 27, 1917, soldiers in several barracks mutinied. The next day the first revolutionary government was already being formed, and on March 2, Czar Nicholas II abdicated. His fate was sealed: the power which had been held for centuries by the Czars of Russia passed into new hands. In the provinces, where news from Petrograd took some time to arrive, there was less tension. Metropolitan Andrew was still living peaceably in retirement at Yaroslav when one morning early in March the police who had been ordered to watch him told him that their weapons had been taken away. Some hours later he learned that the town officials had been thrown into jail. A few days after these events, Father John Deibner and Miss Ushakov arrived unexpectedly and told him of the upheavals in Petrograd and, in particular, that a provisional republican government had been formed under the presidency of Prince Lvov. Finally three weeks after the beginning of the revolution, the Metropolitan was officially informed that he was free.

The situation in the capital had changed in many ways. The new government, anxious to remove the restraints of the old régime, proclaimed a complete amnesty for all religious offenses, and, on March 20, all restrictions on freedom of worship were abolished.

The sense of relief felt by Catholics in Russia can well be imagined. By a happy coincidence, Metropolitan Andrew arrived in Petrograd at the time when this good news was announced. The Catholic community wished to assure him of a warm welcome, and they invited him to celebrate a solemn Liturgy in the church of the Knights of Malta. All the members of the Russian Catholic clergy present in Petrograd took part in the service, and chants were sung by one of the best choirs in the city. During this Liturgy, Metropolitan Andrew ordained to the priesthood Vladimir Abrikosov, who had arrived from Moscow a few days earlier. For the first time in Russian history the newspapers of the capital consented to announce this Catholic ceremony, and as a result the church was crowded.

Vladimir Vladimirovich Abrikosov and his wife Anna Ivanovna had been for some years the center of Russian Catholic life in Moscow where they lived in a huge apartment on the fourth floor of a building on Prechistensky Boulevard. The Abrikosovs were cousins, the members of a rich Muscovite family. Both had received higher educations and Mrs. Abrikosov had studied at Cambridge University. After a period of agnosticism, they had entered the Catholic Church in Paris at the Church of the Madeleine—Anna Ivanovna in 1908, and her husband the following year.

The Abrikosovs had arrived at Moscow in 1910, and their apartment had gradually become a center of study and action in the ancient Russian capital. Every morning the two assisted at the Eucharistic liturgy and received holy Communion; together they strove to increase their religious knowledge, and periodically they arranged in their salon for conferences on dogmatic and ascetic subjects, as also for philosophico-religious meetings at which the Muscovite intelligentsia could exchange their views.

During the summer of 1913 the Abrikosovs went to Rome where they were received in private audience by Pope Pius X. The Pontiff was interested in their work and encouraged them to continue their efforts, giving them a signed photograph of himself as a souvenir of the occasion.

On November 21 of that same year, before leaving Rome, both Mr. and Mrs. Abrikosov became members of the Third Order of St. Dominic. Returning to Moscow, they eliminated every trace of luxury from their existence and kept only one servant. Mrs. Abrikosov gathered around her a select group of young girls—pupils at the conservatory of music, students and young teachers—and taught them Catholic doctrine, the principles of the spiritual life, and endeavored to inspire them with the Dominican ideal. She met with remarkable success, and a certain number of these girls wished, in their turn, to become Tertiaries. Mrs. Abrikosov prepared them,

and they were received into the Order by Father Albert
Lebercier, a French Dominican, who was then in Moscow.

After Vladimir Abrikosov's ordination to the priesthood
by Metropolitan Andrew, he was delegated by Father Louis
Theissling, Master General of the Order of Preachers, to
receive members into the Third Order. A room in the Abrikosov's apartment was transformed into a chapel of the Byzantine rite and became a center of liturgical life for a parish in
the making.

CHAPTER TEN

The New Exarch

In that spring of 1917 Metropolitan Andrew felt that his presence in Petrograd at so crucial a moment in Russian history was providential. Without hesitation he decided to use the powers which had earlier been conferred on him by Pope Pius X to organize the future activities of Russian Catholics.

Evidently it was first necessary to appoint to them a priest who had not been associated with any of the rival groups of the past, and whose moral and intellectual qualities would give him a natural authority. The choice was not difficult; the only possible person for this position was Leonid Feodorov. In a report to the Pope on August 17, 1917, regarding his activities in Russia and the measures he had taken at this historic moment, the Metropolitan wrote: "I have chosen [as Exarch] Father Feodorov because he is the only one of the Catholic priests capable of undertaking this task and because, apart from this, he is truly pious, humble and learned; he is a man of prayer and above all a churchman and a man of Roman spirit. . . ."[1]

According to Byzantine civil and religious law, an exarch

in various circumstances represents the supreme authority in a particular territory. At one time the Byzantine emperors chose an exarch to govern their territory of Ravenna in Italy, and it was through an exarch that the Holy Synod of the Russian Church administered the Orthodox Church in Georgia. The title bestowed on Father Feodorov was the one best suited to define the nature of his office, first because it implied that the widest possible powers had been given to him; then, as it was a Byzantine title, it showed that these powers were given him only over the faithful of the Greek rite; finally, as a new title in the Catholic Church, it contained the idea that this office was to be considered as out of the ordinary and temporary, and that the Exarch of the Russian Catholics would remain in office until the hoped-for corporate reunion between the Russian Church and the Roman Church could be realized.

While these serious decisions were being taken in Petrograd, Father Leonid was still isolated in Siberia. The Metropolitan approached the new Russian Minister of Religion to plead for his release, and this was granted without difficulty. The new Exarch once more crossed the Ural mountains and arrived in Petrograd only a few hours before the celebration of Easter, which fell that year on April 2. He was awaited at the station by no less a personage than Mr. Anton Vladimirovich Kartachov of the Holy Synod. The Catholic community, for its part, held in readiness for him a mitre as well as a gold-plated pectoral cross inspired by an ancient model and designed by Father Gleb Verkovsky.

In the Greco-Russian tradition the Easter office is particularly attractive and uplifting because of the exuberant joy of the chants, the burst of light and the perfume of incense which accompany it, and the actions of the priests and the congregation. But in the year 1917 for the Russian Catholics the ceremony was unforgettable. In previous years it had been held in secret, carried out with subdued voices behind windows shaded with black paper blinds. This year things had changed.

For the first time they could hold the procession which precedes the service. As Metropolitan Andrew was ill, the new Exarch presided. At exactly midnight, the clergy and the faithful with candles in their hands left their chapel through Barmalayeva Street and after a short procession returned through Pushkarskaya Street. When they reached the chapel door, which was still closed, the Exarch and those who were celebrating with him began to sing to an imposing melody, reminiscent of the peal of trumpets, the *troparion* or Byzantine Easter chant: "Christ is risen from the dead. . . ." Then the door was opened, the chapel lighted, and the singing continued while the procession entered. Another sign of the times, adding significance to the ceremony, was the presence of Archbishop Edward Ropp, successor to Archbishop Kliuchinsky as Latin Ordinary of Mohiliov.

"At the end of the Matins," an eye-witness account tells us, "the Exarch, following the rubrics, himself read St. John Chrysostom's Pascal homily. He was deeply moved, and stammered slightly over the first words. But he soon gained control of his emotions and recited the rest of the homily with his usual careful diction and in a strong and melodious voice." [2] The Gospel of the liturgy which followed was sung in Greek, in Latin, in Slavonic and in Russian. Finally, after three hours of chants and prayers, the faithful joined their Exarch and the other priests in breaking the Lenten fast with a feast which lasted until daybreak.

Metropolitan Andrew was confined to bed for three weeks. When he had recovered sufficiently, he decided to summon what he called an eparchial or diocesan synod to draw up with the greatest possible precision the statutes of the young

Russian Catholic Church. The clergy prepared themselves by making a retreat together, and on May 28, 1917, the first Sunday after Pentecost, and All Saints' Day in the Byzantine calendar, the Metropolitan celebrated a Pontifical Liturgy in the Church of the Knights of Malta. After this the first meeting of the synod took place in a room adjoining the Church of St. Catherine; Metropolitan Andrew and seven Russian priests were present on this occasion. At the final session they were joined by three bishops of Latin rite and some priests and laymen. This session was opened by a young priest, Father Diodorus Kolpinsky, who read, first in Russian and then in Latin, the official act establishing the Exarchate of Russia. Then Metropolitan Andrew rose and officially announced the nomination of Father Feodorov to the post of Exarch of Russian Catholics with jurisdiction over the whole of European and Asiatic Russia except the Ukraine and Bielorussia.

These last two regions of the old empire were at this time disturbed by nationalist and separatist movements. Father Feodorov had only a slight knowledge of their special dialects, and the Metropolitan thought that he should not add to the already immense task of the new prelate by confiding these regions to him at this troubled moment in their history. However this restriction was somewhat vague and, as we shall see, it did not prevent the Exarch from intervening in these territories.

The priests of Latin rite as well as those of Byzantine rite who were present at the ending of the synod signed the act establishing the Exarchate. Following this each of the priests of Byzantine rite swore allegiance to the Pope and to the Exarch. In the course of its sessions the eparchial synod of Petrograd had passed resolutions on the discipline of Russian Catholic clergy, the forms of liturgy that were to be used, and the publication of religious works in Russian for Catholics. Unwittingly the government of former Czar Nicholas II had done much to pave the way for Metropolitan Andrew's actions at this crucial moment. Early in September 1914, during the occupation of Lvov by the Russian armies, the imperial government had immediately confiscated from the archives of the archiepiscopal palace all of the Metropolitan's correspondence and documents; these had been piled into trucks and sent to Petrograd, where they were carefully examined by a specialist in Ukrainian questions, Mr. D. Dorochenko. His conclusions were decisive: "The papers confiscated from the Metropolitan," he declared, "are archives of great historical value; they are composed of his private and official correspondence. They do not contain the slightest reference to any revolutionary or terrorist activity." A section of the Okhrana had been ordered to give a report on the documents, and they also declared to the imperial ministry that they gave no grounds for supposing that the Metropolitan had been engaged in political activity.[3]

On this visit in 1917 the Metropolitan was obliged to stay in Russia longer than he had wished, first because of illness and then of an unforeseen delay in obtaining a passport. Before leaving he wished to finish his work by giving episcopal consecration to the priest whom he had placed at the head of the little Russian Catholic community, but in this he met with strong opposition from Father Leonid himself. The Exarch begged him to wait until the Pope had been informed of the decisions taken and had confirmed him in his post. "By this," he said, he "hoped to put his strength to the test before accepting such a responsibility."

They were to wait four years for confirmation from the Holy See. As we have already seen, in 1907 Pope Pius X had felt that he ought to give Metropolitan Sheptitzky exceptional powers in order to assist his eventual pastoral activity in Russia; however he knew that if this came to the knowledge of the imperial government it would have a devastating effect on relations between Russia and the Vatican. As Pius X wished to take full responsibility on himself, he did not inform his Secretariat of State, and consequently there was no record of his decision in the Vatican archives. And the saintly Pope had died in 1914. When, in 1917, the Papal Secretariat of State was informed that Metropolitan Andrew had extended his stay in Russia and that he was organizing the Russian Catholic community there, surprise at his actions was expressed and his right to act in this way outside his ecclesiastical jurisdiction was questioned.

The diplomatic mission from Russia to the Vatican was at this time in the charge of the legation's secretary, Mr. Nicholas Bock. In the memoirs which he published in America in 1960, he tells that Cardinal Gasparri, the Secretary of State, asked him whether he had been informed of the extraordinary powers conferred on Metropolitan Andrew. "We have no record of them, either in the Secretariat or at the Propaganda College," the Cardinal said, and added: "Delegations conferred by word of mouth were quite common in apostolic times, but in the twentieth century it is something unheard of!" [4]

It was only at the end of 1920, after many setbacks, that the Metropolitan was finally able to go to Rome. He arrived on December 16, and was able to explain his actions by showing the documents signed by Pius X in support of the powers he had exercised. Pope Benedict XV then gave his approval of the course the Metropolitan had pursued, and on March 1, 1921 confirmed Exarch Leonid in his post. At the same time he gave the Exarch the title of apostolic protonotary *ad instar*, "so that he should thus be given the dignity appropriate to his office, and to show the special good will of the Holy Father toward him," [5] to quote the terms of the official letter accompanying his appointment.*

In 1917 Russian Catholics enjoyed freedom of worship *in fact,* but it had still not been accorded to them as a *legal right.* Early in June of that year Metropolitan Andrew was in conference with Exarch Leonid when they received an unexpected visit from the second son of Princess Elizabeth Volkonsky, Prince Peter, who had returned from the front on a short furlough. The two prelates were at that moment discussing the most delicate of the problems still left to be solved: how to obtain official recognition for their community from the Provisional Government. They were not sure whether it was wise to make a request for recognition or whether it was better not to attract attention; might not a move of this sort awaken latent animosity and opposition? "I am on friendly terms with Prince G. E. Lvov," Prince Volkonsky told them. "Would you like me to try to win him over to our point of view? At any rate, I could try telephoning the Ministry of the Interior, and ask for a short interview."

The two prelates accepted the suggestion. Luckily Prince Lvov was at the Ministry, and Prince Volkonsky explained over the telephone the subject he wished to discuss with him.

"Would you mind waiting for a few minutes," the official answered, "and I will inquire about it."

Ten minutes later, Prince Lvov himself rang Prince Volkonsky and suggested that Metropolitan Andrew and Exarch Leonid come the following day for an interview.[6]

During this interview a commission presided by Prince

---

* We might note in passing that Mr. Nicholas Bock, the last secretary of the Russian mission to the Vatican before its suppression by the Soviets, himself became a fervent Catholic in Paris nine years later. He was ordained a priest at the age of 67, after the death of his wife in Japan in 1946, and a year later he joined the Society of Jesus. He died in New York at the Russian Center at Fordham University on February 27, 1962.

Lvov and Mr. A. V. Kartachov examined the powers conferred on the Metropolitan by Pope Pius X. Their validity
was recognized and the Exarch, in his capacity as hierarchical
head of the Russian Catholics, was invited to participate in
the commission which had been formed to study the future
position of the Catholic Church in Russia.

By decree of August 8, 1917, the Provisional Government
abolished all restriction on Catholic freedom of worship on
Russian soil and removed the laws that had formerly been
made against Catholicism of Byzantine rite. The Exarch was
promised an annual salary of 4,000 rubles, and his priests
between 1,200 and 1,300 rubles. Finally, the government
offered the Catholic community part of the building which
had been occupied by the Jesuits until their expulsion from
St. Petersburg in the nineteenth century, so that a parish
center could be organized there. Unfortunately, however, the
Provisional Government was overthrown before these promises could be carried out.

Meanwhile Metropolitan Andrew returned to Galicia by
way of Moscow and Kiev. After his departure Exarch Leonid
had to govern the Russian Catholic community alone; he
was at that time thirty-seven years old.

During the five years which he had passed successively in
ecclesiastical studies, in monastic life and in work as an exile
in Siberia, he had ample opportunity to reflect on the special
pastoral work which awaited him and on the problem of unit-
ing the Eastern and Western Churches. From the first he
took a strong position on this: the true Christian solution
to the problem had to be found in a collective reconciliation
of the two Churches, so far as possible through the intermediary of their hierarchies. To try simply to attract a handful of converts from the Orthodox Church showed too restricted a conception of the enormous problem to be solved.

The primary mission of the little group in Petrograd would

be to serve as an example. The million Catholics of foreign extraction who had gradually formed in small groups from Petrograd to Vladivostok were almost entirely alien to Russia in descent, culture and mentality, and involuntarily kept alive the idea among Russians that their Church was a strange and even hostile institution. Under these circumstances it was impossible for a desire for union to spring up and develop. However, in reality these conflicts were merely surface deep and accidental, and it was possible for the Catholic Church to be fully Russian. The Exarch's task was above all not simply to proclaim this in words, but to prove it could be done; he wished to make his tiny Catholic community what he called an 'exemplary cause' for Reunion. This term borrowed from scholastic philosophy was to be used by him time and again to remind his priests and parishioners of the ideal they should set before themselves.

At this time Leonid had five priests to help him in his task. One of them, Father Zerchaninov, was already seventy years old. Increasingly unbalanced in his judgment and in his behavior, he was more of a burden than a help to the Exarch; moreover he was reluctant to accept the authority of a superior so much younger than himself. Father Deibner's health was continually worsening; his nerves could no longer support strain of any sort. Two younger priests, Fathers Gleb Verkovsky and Diodorus Kolpinsky, the second of whom had come from the Latin rite, were obliged to leave Russia after only a few months. During the first years the Exarch's only capable and stable helper was to be Father Vladimir Abrikosov who was in charge of the Catholic parish in Moscow.

Russian Catholics had become noticeably less tense when in 1917 they were given full freedom of worship; as if by magic old subjects of dispute vanished, and Russian, Polish, Lithuanian and French Catholics became united in their optimism. When the eparchial synod had dispersed, Archbishop Edward Ropp of Mohiliov, had made an impromptu speech in which he offered the Exarch his most sincere good wishes and had promised him his fraternal protection and collaboration. More than this, he also offered him the use of the huge church of the Knights of Malta. Father Leonid thought it preferable, however, to decline this offer; at the time he was using a little oratory next to the Church of St. Catherine and he felt altogether at home there. Moreover he would be able to decorate and furnish it as required by the Byzantine rite. In 1917 and 1918 Archbishop Ropp came, dressed in his pontifical robes, to participate in the Russian Easter service. To return this kindness, the Exarch in these same two years was present at the Christmas midnight Mass of the Latins.

Nowhere however did the fraternity of the Byzantine and Latin Catholics show itself in a more concrete fashion than at the Feast of Corpus Christi in 1918. The Eastern Church strongly stresses the mystery of the Eucharist, but it does not practice external veneration of the Blessed Sacrament; the Western Church, on the other hand, developed this devotion as a reaction against heretics in the Middle Ages who denied the Real Presence. So Petrograd for the first time witnessed the procession of Corpus Christi which is particularly dear to the Poles. Archbishop Ropp himself carried the monstrance, and before him marched the Latin clergy preceded by the Exarch and his priests. The members of the Sodality of St. John Chrysostom, recently founded by the Exarch to promote the reunion of the Churches, were at the head of the procession, grouped around their banner. When it reached the burying ground known as the Viborg cemetery, the procession stopped to allow the crowd to take part in the liturgy concelebrated by the Exarch and two of his priests with two deacons. The event caused a sensation in Petrograd.

A short time afterward, Archbishop Edward Ropp was replaced in the See of Mohiliov by Archbishop John Tseplyak, a very virtuous prelate with deep Catholic feeling, who in turn gave his support to the Russian Catholics.

Another hopeful sign was the desire for reform which appeared at this time in the Russian Orthodox Church. The Provisional Government was set up by the "will of the people" to replace the monarchy which had claimed to rule "by divine right." This change completely undermined the juridical organization of this Church as it had been established by Peter the Great. A Church created by the temporal power and fundamentally controlled by it would have looked for its chief support to the new government, but the Russian conscience had instinctively never accepted the synodal administration which Peter the Great had given it. In a surge of vitality, the Church took this historic opportunity and struggled to regain its independent life. In this struggle Catholics saw a definite promise of reconciliation.

The Orthodox Metropolitans of Petrograd and Moscow who owed their election to the intrigues of Rasputin were asked to resign and were immediately replaced. On April 29, 1917, the former imperial synod, now almost entirely filled by new members, decreed the opening of a General Council of the Russian Church to study the problems raised by recent events. The convocation of a Council at this moment was not without certain dangers. Some felt that the democratic ideas which were in favor in politics as a reaction against the absolutism of the monarchy might carry too much weight in ecclesiastical affairs, and certain conservative prelates wanted attendance at the Council to be reserved to churchmen alone. However the majority of the members of the Holy Synod did not agree with them; of the 564 persons who were invited to attend the General Council, 314, or nearly three-fifths, were laymen. Among the ecclesiastics were 80 bishops, 149 priests and 9 deacons.

The Council, or Sobor, was held in Moscow and opened

on August 15, 1917, with impressive ceremonies. While all
the members of the Council took part in a liturgy in the
Cathedral of the Dormition of Our Lady, in the heart of
the Kremlin, a similar service was held for the people in
thirty-three churches of the city. Then the faithful left their
thirty-three churches and met in the Kremlin where a *moleben,* or votive service of supplication, was held before this
immense crowd. On the next day the first public session of the
Council opened in the huge Church of Christ the Savior.

Revolutionary troubles were steadily increasing in Russia,
and made it particularly urgent to establish a strong higher
authority in the Church. On October 11 Archbishop Mitro-
phanus of Astrakhan suggested that the proposed election of a
Patriarch should be studied without further delay. The two
tendencies which had been present among the members of
the Sobor from the beginning now appeared clearly: some
wished to reestablish the Patriarchate which had been suppressed by Peter the Great, while others asked for the Church
to be governed by a synod, elected not as before by the temporal power, but by Councils which would convene officially
at fixed intervals. Finally a compromise was agreed upon, and
it was decided that:

1. In the Russian Orthodox Church, legislative and ju-
dicial powers should belong to the Regional Council which
would meet at predetermined intervals, and be composed of
bishops, clerics (priests and deacons) and laymen. The Council was also to have the power of censure.

2. The Patriarchate was to be reestablished, and the Patriarch would preside over ecclesiastical administration. Although the other bishops would be his equals, he would enjoy
honorary primacy over them.

3. The Patriarch and the ecclesiastical administration as a
whole would be subject to the Council.

Three candidates to the Patriarchate were chosen and, on

the evening of November 4, their names were placed in a box below the historic and miraculous icon of Our Lady of Vladimir. The next day an old blind hermit was chosen to pick the name of the Lord's elected from the box; the name was that of Archbishop Tikhon (Belavine), Metropolitan of Moscow. The new Patriarch was not outstanding for his learning, and his administrative career had not been particularly brilliant; he was first and foremost a pastor. However, he was generally revered, and at the opening of the Council he had been elected president by 407 votes from an electorate of 432.[7]

Exarch Leonid realized the importance of the Council's decisions both for the future of the Russian Church and for its eventual reconciliation with the Catholic Church. Mr. A. V. Kartachov, Minister of Religions, had given him permission to follow the sessions as an observer and he tried to be always in attendance.

Some days after the election of the Patriarch, a speech was made to the Council which gave the Exarch particular pleasure. The speaker was Archpriest Alexander Ustinsky, a master of theology and chaplain in a convent at Novgorod. "The election of the Patriarch," he said, "gives the Russian Orthodox Church an excellent opportunity to make a gesture, however small it might be, toward the other Christian Churches in view of reconciliation. Let the Patriarch then send His Holiness Pope Benedict XV a letter to announce his election, as he has already done to the Eastern Patriarchs. His Holiness the Pope would be pleased and touched by this gesture. What joy and consolation it would bring him! Let us, as Orthodox churchmen, act with due respect toward the Bishop of Rome, as toward the Supreme Pastor of the Christian world, and he will no doubt reply suitably to our fraternal gesture. Who knows? This action on our part may mark the beginning of a new era in relations between the

Catholic and Orthodox Churches. Both of us, surely, are tired of our mutual bad relations. There may be hope that they will soon end; when will we be able to give each other the kiss of peace? What a happy day that will be . . ." [8]

Unfortunately the Fathers of the Council could give only divided attention to this proposal. Even as the Patriarch was being elected the crack of shots and the bursting of shells could be heard nearby. The Bolsheviks were bombarding the Kremlin which was held by a group of *junkers* (pupils of the military school) who were still faithful to the Provisional Government. Political events were growing more and more disturbing, and the Council had to be adjourned without a day being fixed for it to reassemble.

CHAPTER ELEVEN

Amid Chaos

IN October 1905, during the first revolutionary wave in Russia, the workers of St. Petersburg had set up a "Council" in order to direct their movement, and their example was followed by workers of other important cities. The Russian word for council is "Soviet"; it is familiar today throughout the world. At the beginning, these Soviets were nothing more than simple strike committees, but they were soon transformed into political organizations whose leaders met to exchange views and draw up their demands.

In March 1917, during the early days of the Revolution, the Soviets reconstituted the organization of these strike committees, but this time deputies, soldiers and peasants joined the workers' delegates. It was thus that in the capital the Soviet of Petrograd soon became a dominant influence of resistance to the Provisional Government. They held it in check and on October 25 (or November 7 according to the new calendar), definitely overthrew it.

In this Soviet of the capital the extremists known as "Bolsheviks" had gained the upper hand, demanding a radical overthrow of the social order, the dictatorship of the proletariat, the return of the factories to the workers and of the lands to the peasants, and the immediate end of the war. Once in power, they intended to reorganize society according to their own plans.

The result was indescribable chaos throughout Russia. At the front the soldiers mutinied, ceased to fight, disbanded throughout the country, and were often seen drunk and resorting to pillage. The peasants appropriated the lands after driving out and often mistreating the former proprietors. The workers seized the factories. The railroads were completely disorganized. Food, already very scarce in the large cities because of the war, completely disappeared from the markets. Driven by hunger, the city workers rushed to the countryside, pillaging and burning as they went. After being treated in such a manner, the farmers reduced the size of their crops, especially since the city population no longer had anything to offer in exchange for their produce. Often, even at the most critical moments, the government or the army took from them the grain they needed for sowing. Soon famine reigned throughout the land.

After days of hope during the summer and autumn of 1917, Father Leonid experienced five years of privation, struggle and anguish. On May 11, 1918, he wrote to Metropolitan Andrew: "Eighty per cent of our meager resources are used to support our clergy. A pound of sugar sells for 30 rubles . . . the daily ration of bread has fallen to the eighth of a pound." [1] In another letter written in August 1918, he states that three-fourths of his faithful had left the town to escape certain death through famine. One of his deacons, Father Trague, had succumbed to exhaustion and misery. In October the Exarch estimated that scarcely one-seventh of his faithful still remained in Petrograd. At the same period, he wrote to a friend who had sent him some food, "I have received your parcel. . . . Thanks to this kind gesture, I can work hard in the evening and my hands are no longer powerless from exhaustion." [2] But he was forced to admit that parcels sent earlier had not reached him; they had been stolen en route by starving men and women.

During the winter, lack of fuel was added to that of food. Certain specific details in his letters reveal how cruel the winter was in Petrograd. "In January," he wrote, "when there was no wood, the wine froze in the church and the chalice stuck to the lips; it was impossible to bend the fingers to make the sign of the cross [in the Russian manner]." [3] His letters of this period also reveal that, in order to retain a bit of heat in his room and in that of the aged parishioners he had set his heart on helping, the Exarch spent many hours in search of wood on the docks, dragging it to his dwelling and cutting it up with saw and ax. Moreover, he often had to interrupt his work in order to stand in line before shops to collect at an assigned time the rations of sugar, milk, petroleum and other products to which he was entitled.

After their seizure of power, the Bolsheviks had drawn up for the army a manifesto which many soldiers interpreted as an invitation to kill their leaders. Many officers were massacred, but others managed to group themselves and to organize in the north, in the east, and especially in the south of Russia, troops known as White armies whose aim was to overthrow the dictatorship of the Soviets. These armies met with both successes and reverses. On July 16, 1918, at the approach of one of these White armies, composed mostly of former Czech volunteers, the Bolsheviks at Ekaterinburg massacred ex-Czar Nicholas II, his wife and their five children. With a desperation which was often ferocious, this civil war was to be waged at different points on Russian soil for two years more, ending only in November 1920 with the defeat of General Wrangel by the Red troops.

In 1918, the Ukraine had declared its independence of Russia and had been invaded by the Central Powers; in 1920 the Poles, succeeding the Germans, advanced as far as Kiev. In May of that year the Red armies had forced them back as far as the gates of Warsaw, but on August 16 of the same year they were defeated as a result of a Polish counter-offensive. On March 21, 1921, at Riga, the Soviets were forced to sign with Poland a peace treaty with humiliating conditions for Russia. The age-long enmity between Poland and Russia was once again revived.

Civil war and war abroad merely increased the tension, disorders and shortages in the country. "The reason for my long silence," the Exarch wrote to a friend early in 1920 "is the utter lack of free time. We are completely absorbed in the struggle for existence. First hunger and cold, and now other trials; exanthematous typhus is raging and moreover we are without light. Electric current does not come on until nine in the evening, and we have neither petroleum nor candles unless we are prepared to pay exorbitant prices. We don't even have enough candles for the church. In December and January, all my evenings were lost. Fortunately, the clocks have now been advanced an hour. I can read and write; thus today I can send you a letter. Electricity is supplied only every three days and merely for two hours. It is a miracle of divine kindness that I am alive and that our church still exists. A good number of our Russian Catholics have died of starvation. The others have disappeared in every direction in order to escape from cold and hunger." [4]

The two persons who were most dear to the Exarch departed from this world when this chaotic period began for Russia. His mother expired early in May 1918. Her funeral took on the aspect of a manifestation of sympathy toward the Exarch and touched those present to such a point that one entire family requested to be received into the Church. After

Exarch Leonid Feodorov

His last photograph sent from Northern Russia to Bishop Neveu. The inscription under the photo was written on back of the original

Vladimir Soloviov

Metropolitan Andrew Sheptitzky

Prince Peter Volkonsky

Princess Elizabeth Volkonsky

Miss Natalie Ushakov

Father Alexis Zerchaninov

*Leonid Feodorov
at Anagni Seminary*

Leonid Feodorov at Tobolsk   *Father Vladimir Abrikosov*

Mrs. Anna Abrikosov (L) as a young girl
with her cousin Vera

Reprinted with the kind permission of the University of Washington Press, from *St. Petersburg, London, Peking, Tokyo: The Memoirs of Dmitrii Abrikossow*, edited by George Alexander Lensen

Father Dimitri Kuzmine-Karavaiev   *Archbishop John Tseplyak*

*Father
Edmund A. Walsh, S.J.*

*Procession in Petrograd, 1918
Archbishop Feodorov in center (wearing mitre)*

Patriarch Tikhon

The Prisoners in Moscow, Palm Sunday, 1923

Monsignor Budkiewicz speaking during the trial

*Exarch's letter to Father Walsh written from the
prison of Sokolniki, June 4, 1923*

The Monastery of Solovki

much suffering from a stomach abscess, Miss Ushakov died
in the fall of 1918.

In 1921–22, the Exarch's situation became somewhat more
tolerable in certain respects. This was due to the efforts of an
English Catholic, Mr. Leigh-Smith, who resided in Moscow,
and of the Provincial of the English Dominicans, Father Bede
Jarrett.

When, in 1922, the Exarch was able to get a letter to Metropolitan Andrew, he wrote not without a touch of humor:
"During 1918 and 1919 it befell your humble servitor—
Exarch of Russia, Archpriest and Apostolic Protonotary—to
have been so hungry that his arms and knees trembled. Even
now he still has to cut down trees and chop them, reduce
houses and barges to firewood, strike the anvil at the forge,
push wheelbarrows or drag them with loads of wood or gar-
bage, cultivate a vegetable garden and watch over it at night.
The mercy of God alone explains the fact that I am not yet
dead or have not been rendered totally incapable of working
by my anemia and the rheumatism which gnaws at me like a
rat gnaws at an old piece of wood. You must admit that in
such a situation it is scarcely possible to produce anything." [5]

After five years of Soviet régime, thanks to the benevolence
of a traveler the Exarch had an opportunity to send to Pope
Pius XI in Rome a rather long report on the situation of his
Exarchate. This report is dated May 5, 1922. "We have two
main Russia Catholic centers," he wrote, "one at Petrograd,
the other at Moscow. A month ago we were able to begin a
third at Saratov. At Petrograd we have about 70 faithful, at
Moscow about 100; at Saratov, we still have only 15. Moreover, we have more than 200 faithful scattered throughout
the cities and villages of our immense country, for example at
Volgoda, Viatka, Tomsk, Orel and Pensa. Many left Russia
between 1918 and 1920 in order to save their lives or look for
better living conditions. Many have died of hunger or of

different illnesses. The number of those who have thus left us may well reach 2,000." [6]

The Exarch divided his faithful into two groups. A certain number among them had discovered the Catholic Church at one of the most important turning points of their lives, for example at the time of marriage. It happened that when an Orthodox young man married a Catholic girl of the Latin rite, the partner made the following agreement: the Catholic party would follow the Russian liturgical tradition, but both would profess the Catholic faith. Thus each would contribute his most enriching traditions to the new home. These faithful constituted what the Exarch called his "movable group." They were less sedulous at the services. For example, the weather on a Sunday morning merely had to be less favorable for many of these people to assist at Mass in a Catholic church of Latin rite situated closer to where they lived. "This group of faithful," wrote the Exarch, "generally consists of persons of modest social condition: farmers, workers, servants, soldiers, minor employees, businessmen and merchants.

"Other faithful came to the Catholic Church in a very personal manner often as the result of a long and painful religious crisis. In fact, many of them had no religion before their conversion. These neo-converts show a never-failing fidelity and devotion; they are prepared for any sacrifice for the Catholic Church. Eighty percent of these faithful are intellectuals, often members of the ancient nobility of the land." [7]

The Exarch seized the opportunity presented by this letter to enlighten the Holy Father on the following point: "I should like to draw the august attention of Your Holiness to an affirmation which has become current in certain circles who understand nothing of Russian religious questions, or who do not wish to understand them, in order better to deceive the Holy See. They will tell you in substance that when Russians with more refined or higher education think of becoming Catholics, they want only the Latin rite. [They say that] the Eastern rite would be a meager pasture which would attract only more mediocre sheep—peasants and workers, for example. Your Holiness realizes what little basis there is for this affirmation: 90% of the true converts to the Catholic Church of Eastern rite come precisely from the more cultivated society." [8]

Then the Exarch restated for Pius XI the accidental considerations which force certain converts to go over to the Latin rite. He had already explained them, he wrote, to Pope Benedict XV. "A certain number of Russians," he affirmed, "go over to the Latin rite solely because the priest who receives them in the Church does not inform them of the Eastern rites. Others marry Catholics of Polish origin and prefer to adopt their partners' rite. Still others do it out of a kind of reaction against the national Orthodox Church. In the course of their lives they have often met Orthodox priests who are negligent and unable to resist alcohol and human passions; they have turned them away from the religion they represent. Such neo-converts do not want a Catholic rite which is too great a reminder of their former religion. Among the young, especially girls, some are attracted to the Latin rite by the outer beauty of the religious ceremonies (more majestic altar, organ music, great outer piety of the faithful), or by the superior and more Western culture of the clergy." "It is hoped," the Exarch concluded, "that in the future these conditions will carry less and less weight and that the attraction to the Latin rite will exert less and less its fatal influence upon the faithful." [9]

In referring in his letter to the Pope to those intellectuals who were once atheists or agnostics and had become fervent Catholics, the Exarch had particularly in mind a Russian lady, Miss Julia Nicolaevna Danzas, who after her conversion assisted him with remarkable devotion. In a letter of February 1921 to Metropolitan Andrew, the Exarch called her "a great Russian patriot of tremendous erudition." "In the world of scholars," he wrote, "she is considered an eminent specialist in classical philosophy, especially that of Plato. She is known particularly for a major work on the gnostic sects which she published under the pseudonym of Youri Nicolaev. She is now professor of the history of France and England at the Herzen University; she is in charge of incunabula in the public library and is president of the section of the house of scholars. I was a member also; it was there that I met her, and God gave me this soul which was already prepared for Reunion. She was merely waiting for some one to plunge her into the vivifying waters of the Universal Church." [10]

Since 1913, when the Government had officially closed the chapel in Barmalayeva Street, the two veterans of Russian Catholicism, Fathers Zerchaninov and Deibner, had become accustomed to celebrate services at a side altar of the Church of St. Catherine, the main Latin Catholic church of Petrograd. Immediately after his return from Tobolsk, the Exarch followed their example and also lived in the residence next to the church. However, after several months he decided to make a change, preferring to live alone; the two old priests were not always easy to get on with. "So far as Father Zerchaninov is concerned," Miss Danzas reports, "he affected a certain truculence toward the Exarch. Using his seniority as a pretext, he felt his rights of precedence were being encroached upon, not only because of his advanced age but because of the many years since his conversion. This attitude was certainly not designed to lighten Mgr. Feodorov's load which was already very heavy." [11]

Earlier the aged Father Alexis had shown ill humor toward Miss Natalie Ushakov when she had insisted he give up latinizations and retain the Russian rite in all its purity. He

had not forgiven Father Feodorov for having adopted a different attitude from his own and for sharing the views of an old
maid. Several letters he wrote at that time have been saved
in which he constantly returns to the same theme: "It's unfortunate for the Church of God when women begin to
speak. . . ."

"Mgr. Feodorov," Miss Danzas wrote, "avoided as much
as possible using his authority over the seventy-year-old prelate, who, in spite of his eccentricity and sometimes discon-
certing whims, was really very good-hearted, thus excluding
any possible hostility on his part or toward him.

"As for Father Deibner, exhausted by his earlier work and
especially by family responsibilities, his spells bordered on
neurasthenia. In his attitude toward the Orthodox, the in-
temperance of his language aroused the indignation of his
hearers and created serious problems for the Exarch." [12]

We are indebted to Miss Danzas also for a rather detailed
description of the oratory where the Exarch usually celebrated
services during these five years. "The small church in Barmalayeva Street," she wrote, "was not a separate building, but
simply a room arranged in a private dwelling which had been
that of Father Deibner. The two-story wooden house was
small. The first floor was occupied by tenants who were never
seen; the other floor had a separate entrance with a staircase
leading directly into the church, that is, into a small anti-
chamber where candles or small loaves of bread (prosphora)
were sold to the faithful who offered them to the priest before
the Liturgy. From this, one entered the church itself which
occupied the space of two rooms transformed into one; at the
far end, opposite the entrance, was the iconostasis. Four windows of the church faced Barmalayeva Street. Two others, at
the far end of the sanctuary, faced Pushkarskaya Street. To the
right of the sanctuary, another small room served as sacristy."

The iconostasis and the ikons which covered it were the

work of amateurs, and the chapel revealed the humblest poverty. Yet during the hours of service, especially on Sunday and holidays, it was always crowded. In addition to the small Catholic community, many Orthodox were seen. They stated that the services were more beautiful than in their own churches. "Of course, it was not the outer beauty that impressed them," Miss Danzas wrote, "but the way in which Father Feodorov conducted the service, the profound faith which emanated from his every gesture and word and which contrasted with the negligence frequent in the Russian parish churches, especially during the time of the great *débâcle*."

"The love of God," she continues, "and the ardent faith of the Exarch were clearly evident in his way of celebrating the Holy Liturgy. It was especially this which won souls. As a preacher he was not always within the reach of his listeners; a profound theologian, he often found it difficult to put himself on the level of a roomful of simple people. Yet in his way of speaking there was a kind of sacred fire which drew the listeners beyond their ordinary level.

"I recall the deep impression he made one day on a huge crowd at the Church of St. Catherine by a sermon applying to the Church the parable of the grain of mustard seed. This sermon resulted in several conversions, and I remember a woman saying to me with tears in her eyes, 'Ever since Father Leonid explained so well the great tree of God which is ever growing and the small branches which are sprouting with the small leaves, I also want to be one of these small leaves.'

"As a confessor Mgr. Feodorov was wonderful, and everyone who had occasion to lay his soul bare before him has retained the loving memory of the wholehearted way in which he gave himself to this ministry, the spiritual compassion with which he shared the penitent's anguish of doubt or pain. It is true, however, that some accused him of being too severe, but it was always because he showed himself to be inflexible on questions regarding marriage, divorce and matrimonial problems on which the Russians are accustomed to a culpable indulgence which Mgr. Feodorov reproved and to which he opposed the inalterable doctrine of the Catholic Church." [13]

The Russian Catholic community of Moscow was somewhat more numerous than that of Petrograd and centered entirely around Father Vladimir Abrikosov and his wife, Anna Ivanovna, in their apartment on Pretchistensky Boulevard. It was now not only a parish but a religious community, sheltering a number of the young girls whom Mrs. Abrikosov had interested in the Dominican spirituality.

The passage of these young girls to Catholicism had often met with violent opposition on the part of their families, and several of them had been forced to leave home. Mrs. Abrikosov offered them hospitality, and her home had taken on the aspect of a small convent; the girls continued their work or studies outside, but fulfilled their devotional exercises and followed the practices of religious life at night when they were together in the apartment. On February 19, 1921, the Master General of the Dominicans transformed a *de facto* situation into one *de jure:* he raised the community to the rank of Religious of the Third Order, that is, they became Dominicans proper. By 1922 the number of these Dominicans was slightly over 20, the maximum number which the apartment could hold. Mrs. Abrikosov, now Mother Catherine of Siena, had been named prioress and Father Vladimir fulfilled the duties of chaplain.

The Exarch who, we will remember, had first visited the Abrikosovs on his hurried trip to Russia in 1914,* followed the activity of the convent and parish of Moscow with his usual discretion. He left Father Vladimir Abrikosov com-

* See p. 94.

pletely in charge. On Christmas Day 1920, a Muscovite priest ordained in the Orthodox Church, Father Serge Soloviov, nephew of the well-known philosopher, requested to be received in the Catholic Church. In 1922, a Russian Catholic of Moscow, Nicholas Alexandrov, received sacerdotal ordination and became Father Vladimir's assistant. He had a degree in electrical engineering and was outstanding not only for his intellectual qualities but also for his zeal.

During this time, Father Abrikosov often met Nicholay Alexandrovich Berdyayev, a writer whose works were soon to enjoy great success in the West. According to his biographer, Donald A. Lowrie, Berdyayev thought very highly of the Abrikosov community and admired the profound spiritual and ascetic life which reigned there.[14] Lydia Berdyayev, his wife, had first been attracted to Catholicism some twelve years earlier while reading the life of St. Teresa which her sister Eugénie had sent her from Paris. Stricken with a serious case of pneumonia, she attributed to the saint her restoration to health. She made a profession of Catholic faith at the home of Father Abrikosov, her husband allowing her complete liberty in the matter.

During the pleasant soirées which took place at that time at the Berdyayev's home, Father Vladimir Abrikosov also met a publicist, Dimitri Vladimirovich Kuzmine-Karavaiev, the son of a professor of law at the University of St. Petersburg. Gifted with superior intelligence and possessing an exceptional memory which made him a walking encyclopedia, this idealistic writer was above all noted for an unselfishness which endeared him to everyone. He had led a rather agitated youth and during his law studies at the University of St. Petersburg had become an active member of the Bolshevik section of the Social-Democratic party. By this very fact, he had declared himself a convinced atheist. Suspected of subversive activity, he was arrested by the Czarist police and during the autumn of 1907 submitted to a cure of solitude in prison. The cure was salutary. Having completed his studies, he sought public employment. In spite of the distinctly unfavorable dossier furnished by the special police, Alexander Rittich, Director of the Department of State Properties at the Ministry of Agriculture, admitted him to his service after having received his word of honor that he would cease all subversive activity.

But it was Dimitri Kuzmine-Karavaiev's good heart which finally brought him back to Christ; in fact, his kindness was outstanding. One day in 1913 he was returning from Tambov to St. Petersburg when a poor woman went through the railroad carriage selling the New Testament to the travelers. As she had met with no success and appeared very unhappy, the young lawyer took pity on her and bought a book. "I did it," he relates in his *Memoirs*, "partly out of compassion and partly also out of snobbery." On his return to St. Petersburg, his mother wanted to put his briefcase in order, knowing only too well that her son's brilliant and speculative mind did not linger on details of order and regularity. With a smile which expressed her utter joy, she said, "I didn't know, Mitya, that you carried the New Testament among your papers!"

Her son was a bit embarrassed, but he kept the little book to please his mother, and did not open it until five years later. What he read came as an overwhelming discovery. Later he wrote: "How many moments of consolation do I owe to that New Testament! The image of Christ the Savior, His winning humility, His love of God and men, so profound and impartial, are forever engraved in my heart."

Father Abrikosov invited him to the theological reunions which were held at his home, and he at once became one of the most well-liked and eloquent members. He soon realized that it was impossible to accomplish fully the will of Christ without entering into communion with the Bishop of Rome. Miss Anastasia Vassilievna Selenkov, a Moscow parishioner, took to heart the task of replying to those considerations by which he sought to justify delay in taking action. She was successful, and on May 5, 1920, the able publicist made a profession of Catholic faith, then received the Eucharist from the hands of Father Abrikosov, Madame Berdyayev assisting at the ceremony.[15] Meanwhile the new Catholic continued to earn his living, working for the Commissar of Agriculture under orders from Joseph Stalin, who was to become the dictator of Soviet Russia.

The third Russian Catholic center, which was begun at Saratov by Father Alexis Onesimov in 1922, counted only some 15 families. Famine and persecution prevented its development.

Civil war had scarcely ended when a new calamity, this time caused by nature herself, inflicted extreme suffering on the Russian people. During the summer of 1921, a catastrophic drought occurred in the Volga basin, affecting in varying degrees districts that should normally have been granaries for the rest of Russia. In addition, elsewhere the peasants, in a protest against Communist policies, had sown only what crops they considered strictly necessary for their families and relatives. These reduced crops produced no surpluses, and the result was a frightful famine which tortured 37 million human beings and caused the death of about 5 million.

Patriarch Tikhon of the Russian Orthodox Church sent a personal message to the Pope, the Eastern Patriarchs, the Archbishop of Canterbury and the Protestant Episcopal Bishop of New York requesting their aid; the writer Maxim Gorky launched an appeal to the American people. The American government responded generously, appointing a relief commission under the direction of Herbert Hoover.

The Holy See also decided to send a mission to the aid of

the Russians. After examining the situation, Rome realized that the best means of utilizing the funds collected in the Catholic world would be to affiliate the Pontifical Mission with the American Relief Administration, thus coordinating effort and reducing administrative expenses. The Americans were favorable to this project and asked merely that the director of the Pontifical Mission be an American. A young Jesuit born in Boston, Father Edmund A. Walsh, was then at Paray-le-Monial in France for the year of ascetical studies and exercises which is spent by the Jesuits after their ordination. In February 1922, he was summoned to Rome and charged with organizing the Papal relief expedition to the famine-stricken Russians.[16]

In Moscow satisfaction at this announcement was mingled with bitterness and fear, as is testified in the letter of Mother Abrikosov to her friend Princess Marie Volkonsky. "According to an Orthodox priest close to our friends," she wrote at that time, "Patriarch Tikhon was greatly hurt by the response of the Holy Father, and his kindness to us has been dampened. The fact is that Benedict XV answered only through the intermediary of Cardinal Gasparri to the personal letter which the Patriarch had sent, covered with all the seals. The Patriarch took this as a mark of pride and was hurt. The Orthodox priest could not help but exclaim with sadness, 'Now where is the famous diplomacy of the Holy See?' In fact, it was a colossal *faux pas;* Rome must accept the fact that the Russian Church, with Patriarch Tikhon at her head, is a poor and suffering relative and her opulent sister should give her tender and sisterly attention. It is quite important that Pope Pius XI write a beautiful letter of sympathy to Patriarch Tikhon. If it were personal and transmitted by the Exarch, it would produce the best effect." [17]

Moreover, the mission was directed by Jesuits! When Moscow learned this, the people's imagination, heightened by

many years of tension and suffering, immediately visualized
the Pontifical Mission as a new Trojan horse destined to
introduce into Moscow those whom a legend, not only tenacious but grotesque, represented as the most fearful enemies
of the nation. "Does Rome realize," again wrote Mother
Abrikosov, "the terror and repulsion felt here until recently
for the Jesuits and the strange mood in which their arrival is
awaited? It is something inexplicable, a characteristic trait of
panic. If the Jesuits enter Russia in civilian dress, it will mean
only the worst: their arrival here will be considered a gigantic
Catholic conspiracy. One must thoroughly understand the
psychology of the Russian attitude toward the Jesuits. In spite
of my entire respect for this religious Order, I must admit
that it cannot enter Russia. Its arrival here will be the ruin
of all that has been accomplished." [18]

Rome dismissed these apprehensions and in March 1922
Father Walsh made his first trip to Russia to gain an idea of
the situation, to consult competent persons and to draw up
his relief plans. He next went to New York in order to affiliate
the Pontifical Mission with the American Relief Administration, to be certain of the massive shipment of supplies, and to
recruit a team of assistants. He returned to Moscow charged
with a double mission: that of director of the Pontifical Mission for aid to the starving Russians and as the official representative of Catholic interests in Russia to the Soviet government, which had become more and more antireligious. He
considered his first task more urgent and accomplished it in a
masterly manner. Nothing less than the organizing genius of
this American was needed to manage the situation. In a
country where distance had held Napoleon at bay, where the
roads were battered and the railroads paralyzed, where the
government was hostile, although he did not speak Russian
he had to order the transportation of thousands of tons of
supplies; to organize depots, kitchens and refectories. He

accomplished all this and in a few weeks thousands of famished people, especially children, were able to salvage what remained of their strength in canteens established at different points in the most stricken areas. Parcels of food, clothing and medicine were distributed to many families. Thanks to this massive organization, the best possible use was made of the $750,000 collected in the churches of the Catholic world and especially in those of the United States.

On October 10, 1922, Exarch Feodorov was in Moscow and Father Walsh came to see him. This was their first meeting. "Our conversation," Father Leonid wrote, "lasted for two hours. We spoke in Latin and separated as great friends. Father Walsh promised to come to Petrograd in fifteen days. He brought with him provisions for our religious; he promised two parcels of supplies for Father Onesimov (in Saratov) and one for our Sisters (in Petrograd). This good son of St. Ignatius has taken upon himself to procure all the books I need . . . I explained the purpose of our mission. First, he listened calmly, then became more and more enthusiastic over our projects. He understands our situation vis-à-vis the Poles and, in general, our special vocation. He is ready to use all his influence to help us. In short, the success of my interview with him was so surprising that once again I kneel and thank Divine Providence for having sent us such unexpected help." [19]

Won over to the Exarch's ideas, Father Walsh and his Salesian and Jesuit aids took it specially upon themselves to furnish supplies for the Orthodox clergy in the areas where starvation was rampant. At Orenburg, for example, Father Louis Gallagher, S.J., received at his table the six Orthodox bishops then present in the city.

"Father Walsh and I are living in perfect understanding; he helps us as much as he can," the Exarch later wrote to Metropolitan Andrew.[20]

CHAPTER TWELVE

Work for Unity

In the long letter already mentioned, dated May 5, 1922, and addressed to Pope Pius XI, the Exarch clearly explained the objective for which he was working. "Our aim," he wrote, "is to develop the idea itself of Union of the Churches (as we usually say here), to enter into relations with the clergy separated from Rome, to give Russian society an objective picture of the Catholic Church and its holy doctrine. The soul should above all be prepared to grasp the idea itself of Church Unity; first of all, the Russian people must rid themselves of tremendous prejudices against the Catholic faith. Only after this has been achieved can the controversial questions regarding Reunion be discussed.

"When it is a matter of spreading Catholic doctrine in Russia, it should not be overlooked that Catholicism for a Russian is not only a Christian doctrine different from that of the Orthodox Church but also a foreign importation, an importation above all Polish, that is, coming from a detested adversary which during the entire course of Russian history has only caused serious trouble for our people. For this reason, just as an Englishman cannot be a missionary in Ireland, so a Pole cannot cross the Russian frontier as an apostle of Reunion." [1]

To the reader these remarks about Poland will seem harsh and unjust, above all on the part of the Exarch. Poland's sufferings during the past two centuries remain too vivid in this reader's mind; he has not forgotten how that country without natural defenses was divided by its three powerful neighbors, nor the bloody repressions of the Poles who wanted to regain their independence. All the small Polish colonies which extended from Petrograd to Vladivostok were evidence of the violent deportations from Polish territory during the preceding century. Obviously the Exarch was expressing the judgments which he heard around him and which reflected the Russian mentality. The Russians do not easily forget that the Poles occupied the western regions of their country for two centuries and that they had to fight continually against them. It has been a tragedy in the history of the Christian world that these two Slavic nations, representing the Eastern and Western Christian cultures, have been constantly at odds during the centuries.

It must also be remembered that the Exarch wrote these lines only fourteen months after the armies coming from Moscow had been defeated before the gates of Warsaw by the army of a newly independent Poland. Moreover, victorious Poland had annexed a part of White Russia inhabited by a highly mixed population.

The Russian soul was embittered. Moreover, disorder reigned in Russia: divisions were seen in the Russian Church, and by that very fact the Latin Catholic clergy, most of whom were Polish, felt itself somewhat avenged for the religious discrimination from which they had suffered earlier. Some of its members could not rid themselves of a certain triumphalism which prevented them from approaching the religious problem of Russia with the necessary humility and charity.

"In the name of all the Russian Catholics and in that of the Orthodox who are becoming more and more favorable to union with the Roman Church," Father Leonid continued, "I implore Your Holiness to give his august attention to this major obstacle and use all his apostolic authority and liberty to end once and for all the Poles' efforts to intervene in our affairs.

"The method which we are using to practice this apostolate," he continues, "is not exactly active proselytism (although it does not exclude this), nor a noisy propaganda. We are trying to spread our ideas quietly. A few years ago, we published a small review for the general public entitled *Slovo Istini*, but in 1918 it was forbidden like all the other newspapers and reviews which do not comply with the infallibility of the Communist doctrine. Our preaching and conferences, either in the church or elsewhere, have always an irenical character and do not offend the religious feeling of the Orthodox. Canon 52 of our diocesan council held at Petrograd in 1917 stipulates, 'We impose it as a duty to preach sermons on a dogmatic, moral or liturgical theme. In these sermons it is fitting first of all to explain the positive part of the Catholic doctrine and enter only rarely into controversy.' "[2]

The Polish clergy enjoyed focusing attention on the inadequacies of the Russian Orthodox Church, on the failings of its clergy and of its members. Father Leonid preferred to consider the positive values which the Russian Church possesses and encourages. "Like any conquered people thrown into misery," he wrote to Pope Pius XI, "the Russians are becoming more and more jealous of their national dignity. It is true that atheism has made great strides in Russia; it is also true that the clergy separated from Rome greatly suffers from disorganization; but at the same time we see that many Russians who once were only slightly interested in their Church or not at all, have today become devoted and affectionate sons. The eternal law of history verifies this once again: the darker the night, the greater seems the sun's splendor. The waves of mysticism rise all the higher the lower they have been engulfed by the whirling troubles of materialism. More than 2,000 Orthodox priests (their number is ever increasing) and 20 bishops have been shot or massacred by the Bolsheviks. More than half of them are real martyrs; they have fallen victim to the hatred against religion cloaked under the pretense that they were conspiring against the government. Today, the Russian people feel themselves much more Christian than in Czarist times. Indifference, which was then its greatest fault, has disappeared. Whereas formerly a Russian was completely indifferent to his pastor and his parish, today he shows a lively interest in both. At present, the priests are becoming more than ever the heroes of the real national ideal, always united, however, to the Orthodoxy now persecuted by Jews and Communists. The Patriarch, as was the case in Byzantium, somewhat replaces the dignity of the Sovereign. The halo of a confessor of the faith (he is still being watched by the police) invests him with a veneration in the common people's imagination.

"These [Orthodox] priests who formerly seemed to have been struck by dumbness, are today preaching quite well and teaching the Christian doctrine. Under the auspices of some churches, women have also organized study centers where religious subjects are being taught in a very simple manner: Holy Scripture, history of the Church, patrology, dogmatic and moral theology, apologetics and liturgy. Needless to say, similar activity does not exist in the villages or in the smaller towns, and yet once ignited, the flame of religious fervor spreads rapidly everywhere. If in 1918 and 1919 the people remained indifferent to the profanations of the holy relics perpetrated by the Bolsheviks, today they oppose and protest, often to the point of shedding their blood, against the plundering of the churches."

Alluding to certain information published abroad and reprinted by the Russian press, the Exarch exclaimed: "And it is this people, totally impregnated with the Christian idea, even if somewhat distorted or mutilated, whom our dear Poles want 'to convert' as if they were dealing with an African tribe! When last year—no one knows why—a rumor began to spread that, instead of the diocese of Mohiliov, the Holy See was to establish apostolic vicariates in Russia, the decision was interpreted as a great offense to the nation. 'So—!' people said, 'Rome considers us as pagans: all we deserve to have are apostolic vicars!' " [3]

The Catholic parishes of the Latin rite scattered throughout Russia, Europe and Asia did not represent what the Russian Orthodox communities would really become if they entered into communion with the Holy See of Rome: they displayed too foreign a character. Therefore, the Exarch tried to develop his Catholic centers of Petrograd, Moscow and Saratov above all to show as perfectly as possible on a small scale what Union would be like if it could take place.

To believe in the truth and divinity of the Roman Catholic Church is to believe that, in His love for His Church, Jesus Christ confided to St. Peter and to the Bishops of Rome who were Peter's successors, a supreme pastoral and doctrinal mission in order better to assure the unity of the Church and her transcendence beyond the divisions of men. With regard to human freedom, God wills that in every act of faith there be enough light to make the faith reasonable, but He allows sufficient darkness to remain so that the faith be meritorious. These lights and shadows vary according to those who see them and to the circumstances in which they live. It is easy to imagine, for example, that when the Crusaders sacked Constantinople, the inhabitants acquired a view of the Roman primacy in which there were more shadows than lights.

Contrary to this, the disorder which reigned in Russia after the Bolshevik Revolution and the persecutions suffered by Christians, indirectly threw a stronger light on the advantages of organic union with the rest of the Christian world, especially with the Bishop of Rome. Christ's loving kindness, which prompted the establishment of the primacy of the Pope, began to emerge with greater clarity. Better than anyone else, the Exarch realized that the time was particularly favorable to work for the reestablishment of Christian unity.

This thirst for unity was revealed in different ways. Only a few months after the Revolution, a unique case occurred in which an entire Christian community, that is a parish led by its pastor, the monk Potapii, joined the Catholic Church. The experience is worth describing in detail, as it helps understand the practical difficulties encountered by similar undertakings.

Before receiving the monastic tonsure, Father Potapii was known as Peter Emelianov. He was born in 1889 in the Government of Ufa into a family of Old Believers without priests and known for this reason as *Bezpopovtzy*. When he was nine years old, his father was brought back to Orthodoxy by the Bishop of Ufa at that time, the famous Anthony Krapovitzky who afterward became the leader of a group of Russian bishops in the emigration. Transferred to Volhynia, Bishop Anthony took with him young Peter, conferred the monastic tonsure on him and sent him to Jitomir to study theology. When the young monk reached the age of 22, he ordained him priest. In 1916, Bishop Anthony was named archbishop of Kharkov. Again he took Father Potapii with him and in March 1917, committed to him the important parish of Nizh-

naya Bogdanovka, near Lugansk. Bogdanovka is a village of
Great Russians speaking the language of Moscow, who were
transplanted to this part of the Ukraine at the end of the seventeenth century in order to set up an outpost against the raids
of the Tartars from the Crimea.

During his studies, the young monk became an avid reader
of the Fathers of the Church. Like Father Zerchaninov before
him, alone and without the aid of any Catholic priest, he
became convinced that it was impossible to belong wholly
to the Church of Christ without being in communion with the
Bishop of Rome. A zealous and persuasive speaker, he managed after five years of effort to communicate his conviction
to most of his parishioners. He went to Lugansk and revealed
his desire for union with the Roman Church to Father
Mikhail Yagulov, a Georgian priest, the pastor of the sole
Catholic parish of the city. The latter received him cordially
and advised him to explain his case to the regional Catholic
dean at Kharkov, Father Anthony Kviatkovsky. It was there
that Father Potapii learned of the recent foundation of the
Exarchate. On his return to Bogdanovka, he announced his
discovery and his intention to go at once to Petrograd to
place himself under obedience to the Exarch.

The trip was very dangerous. Kharkov was still in the
hands of the Germans; Briansk, somewhat to the north, was
already in the hands of the Soviets. His trip lasted an entire
month. At Petrograd he found the Exarch who was still living
in the building beside the Church of St. Catherine. He presented his request along with a petition signed by the principal families of his parish.

The Exarch kept Father Potapii with him for a few days,
questioned him in detail, made several recommendations and
finally acceded to his request. On June 29, 1918, he received
his profession of faith in the Church of St. Catherine and
celebrated with him the Eucharistic sacrifice. He promised

him also that Father Gleb Verkhovsky, a priest of Petrograd, would soon visit Bogdanovka in his name.

Father Potapii headed south. During the four weeks of his absence, some priests of the neighboring Orthodox parishes had attempted in vain to stir up the parishioners against their pastor. The enemies of Reunion then accused Father Potapii of being a Communist agent; they summoned troops of the Ukrainian army led by General Skoropadsky, then occupying the region, and demanded a punitive expedition against Bogdanovka. When these troops invaded the village, some of the frightened parishioners gave in. The majority, however, remained faithful to Father Potapii. On his return from Petrograd the pastor was enthusiastically received by those who had remained attached to him.

Father Gleb Verkhovsky came several days later, bringing an antimension * and a letter from the Exarch. Then the whole thing was almost ruined. Accustomed to letters printed on fine paper, such as those sent by bishops in the time of the Czars, the peasants were disconcerted by the Exarch's hand-written letters on ordinary paper. The antimension bore the seal of Metropolitan Sheptitzky: in the center, a horseshoe transpierced by an arrow; above, the large hat of a Latin bishop with its hanging tassels. They asked: Why this strange hat? Why this horseshoe and arrow on church paper? A still more serious problem also disturbed them. They thought, "If Father Potapii falls ill, what will become of us? Where will we go for Communion? The Orthodox priests would refuse to accept us."

Father Verkhovsky spent many a long hour explaining and reassuring them. Then, on August 14, 1918, he left Bog-danovka for Kiev, Lvov, then Constantinople.

After his departure, the parish underwent every kind of

* The piece of silk containing relics of saints and blessed by a bishop which corresponds in the Byzantine rite to the altar stone in the Latin rite.

trial, partly as a result of the civil war. Two missionaries sent from Kharkov, accompanied by police, challenged Father Potapii to a public disputation. During the discussion they tried to prove their theses by quoting the Old Believers. But some Old Believers assisting at the oratory contest sided with Father Potapii and the two missionaries lost face.

Meanwhile the Germans again occupied the region. Father Potapii was denounced as a Communist; this was the second time. Together with some other influential citizens he was arrested, beaten and treated so badly that he had to be transported to the Lugansk hospital. Father Yagulov came to see him, explained his case to the Germans and obtained a safe-conduct for him to return to Bogdanovka.

On September 25, 1918, the Orthodox auxiliary bishop of Kharkov, Mgr. Neophyte, arrived in the village with a detachment of 50 soldiers. Many inhabitants fled. Those who remained listened to the bishop who, tears in his eyes, pleaded with them to return to the faith of their ancestors. Nevertheless, they remained faithful to their pastor.

At the end of October, Bogdanovka fell into the hands of the White armies. Again accused of being a crypto-Communist, Father Potapii was confined to the Starobielsk prison where he remained until December 27. On that day the Red armies occupied the city and opened the prison gates. After his release Father Potapii enjoyed seven months of relative peace in his parish. Then in October 1919, the White armies of General Denikin made a new advance in the region. Father Potapii was again confined to the same prison. On November 19, he was transferred to that of Lugansk. On December 24, 1919, the Bolsheviks occupied the city and liberated the prisoners.

At Bogdanovka he was to meet with new difficulties concerning the church building. One part of the inhabitants declared themselves to be Orthodox, the other Catholic. The question arose: to whom henceforth does the church belong? The dispute was referred by the Bolsheviks to the People's Commissar of Justice. Considering that first, 160 families declared themselves to be Catholic, 62 Orthodox and 40 indifferent, and second, that the Orthodox had another place of worship in the village whereas the Catholics did not, the Commissar attributed the church to the Catholics.

The village found itself sharply divided. Those families which had been turned out threatened to set fire to the building. "Such an attitude is in opposition to the Christian spirit," Father Potapii wrote some weeks later in a letter to Metropolitan Sheptitzky, and we "thought it preferable to give up the church. We then began to assemble in a private house, rather ill fitted to our purpose, it is true. Nevertheless, it is better to give up a material possession for a spiritual benefit. Moreover, we hope to build a church with our own means." [4] However, some terrible trials from without came like a steam roller to crush all local quarrels: the Communist taxes, the ruin of the farmers, famine and every kind of religious persecution. The pastor of Bogdanovka was once again arrested. When in the mid-summer of 1918, at Petrograd, Father Feodorov and Father Potapii had fraternally embraced before separating, they had been unable, of course, to foresee that they would not meet again until eight years later, in an island of the White Sea, both condemned to the same forced labor in the ice of the Great North.

Because of slow transportation, high prices and the many steps which had to be taken in order to obtain permission to go from one place to another, the Exarch made a rule not to travel except to Moscow. The sole exceptions to this rule were two trips to Mohiliov in 1922.

The entire region where this city is located, that is, White Russia, became Catholic in 1596 when the Union with Rome was signed at Brest-Litovsk. It was then part of the Polish-Lithuanian kingdom. Later these regions again came under Russian political rule. In 1839, the Union was denounced by certain bishops chosen by the Russian government, and the faithful, whether they liked it or not, were detached from Rome and replaced under obedience to the Holy Synod at Petrograd. In 1905, at the time of the publication of the edict of toleration, several thousands of the faithful again went over to Catholicism; but as the Catholic Byzantine rite was then proscribed in Russia, they had to adopt the Latin one.

In 1922 the dean of Mohiliov was Father Joseph Bielogolov, a White Russian priest, former professor of theology at the Catholic seminary of Petrograd. He had met Father Leonid in Moscow, was won over to his projects and had promised him complete cooperation. In June 1922, he sent a telegram inviting the Exarch to Mohiliov for the feastday of St. Anthony of Padua, patron saint of his parish. The veneration of a miraculous image of the saint, which was kept in the church, usually attracted a huge crowd. Father Leonid set out. The railroad ticket cost him no less than 15 million rubles! A dollar was then worth practically two million rubles.

Father Bielogolov did his utmost to have the Exarch received as an important personage. Twice he had him celebrate the Divine Liturgy in his church and the third time in the small town of Sophiisky, 18 miles from Mohiliov. He made arrangements for him to preach four times. The Exarch was the central figure at all the ceremonies; a place of honor was assigned to him in the choir during the celebration of the services of the Latin rite. Before mounting the pulpit, the different preachers came forward to ask his blessing as they would of a bishop. "The people's surprise on seeing an Orthodox priest surrounded by so much consideration in a Catholic church," the Exarch wrote after these festivities, "exceeds all bounds." [5] But when someone explained to them that the Exarch was a Catholic their astonishment was transformed into great delight. "The Union has returned" was repeated from mouth to mouth with equal joy among Orthodox and Catholics.

Two Orthodox priests and a deacon attended the liturgy which the Exarch celebrated on June 13. A place of honor had been reserved for them. Furthermore, an Orthodox priest and a deacon came to attend the liturgy at Sophiisky where Orthodox and Catholics shared in the prayers and ceremonies celebrated at the church and the cemetery. "The interest in Reunion," wrote the Exarch, "reached such a height that after my Liturgy of June 18, a deputation of White Russian intellectuals came to thank me for the service and sermons and asked me to renew their joy by returning to see them. They begged me not to forget that they all wanted to see the reestablishment of the Union as soon as possible." [6]

After this trip, the Exarch requested with greater insistence at Rome the approbation and diffusion of a prayer for Christian unity which could be used without reservation by both non-Catholics and Catholics. Too often prayers throughout the Catholic world were not acceptable to the Orthodox because they seemed to presuppose their acceptance of the primacy of the Bishop of Rome. Union in a single fervent prayer would be an important step toward Reunion itself. The Exarch wanted the prayer to be short, clear, and intelligible to all. Without presuming to impose it, he suggested the following:

"Cast a glance, compassionate Lord Jesus, our Savior, on the prayers and supplications of Your sinful and unworthy servants who in all humility kneel before You, and unite us all in the one and only Holy, Catholic and Apostolic Church. Shine Your never declining light into our souls. Dissipate the disorders of the Church. Grant us the grace to glorify You

*as a single heart and a single mouth so that everyone may
recognize that we are your true disciples and beloved children.*

*"Merciful Lord, fulfill Your promise without delay that
there may be only one flock and a single pastor in Your
Church and that we may be worthy of glorifying Your Holy
Name, now and forever. Amen."* [7]

In November 1922, the Exarch returned to Mohiliov where
he was again greeted with enthusiasm. On that occasion he
suggested to Father Bielogolov that he go over to the Byzantine rite and continue his apostolate for Reunion in White
Russia. But the dean of Mohiliov did not think the proposi-
tion was timely. "If I leave my post to work exclusively for the
apostolate in favor of Reunion," he explained, "the Poles will
send a priest here who will hamper all our efforts and raise
the people against us."

Another solution would have been to allow the same
priests, and in this case Father Bielogolov, to celebrate either
in the Latin or Byzantine rite according to the need. This
"multi-ritualism" existed, it seemed, before the separation of
the Churches. Mgr. Ropp, former archbishop of Mohiliov,
had been the ardent defender of a similar project, but the
Exarch had refused to support him unless the bi-ritualist
priests were totally withdrawn from the jurisdiction of the
Polish bishops. "It is inadmissible," he wrote in reference to
this subject, "that Russians [in Russia] be governed by Poles."
Nevertheless he thought that such bi-ritualism could be
envisaged if the priests in question were directed by Russian bishops. The real solution, he thought, would be to
grant this faculty to a few priests who would receive the
desirable psychological and intellectual preparation for this
task. [8]

It seemed that no one at that time realized the oppression
to which every religion in Russia was to be subjected by the

Soviets, nor the isolation in which the country would be kept
for some dozen years. The Exarch's letters at that period show
that he hoped for the aid of priests from abroad in his own
apostolate. Above all, he wanted a monastic foundation of the
Benedictine Fathers or of the Camaldolese, whose way of life
was so similar to that of the Eastern monks. He wanted some
Dominicans, also some Jesuits to organize schools and retreat
houses, but after careful consideration he thought that the
Jesuits, at least in the beginning, should follow the Latin
rite. The people had retained too many prejudices against
them to believe in their sincerity if they adopted the Byzantine rite. They first had to prove their real devotion to the
Russian people.[9]

When antireligious persecution became intensified in
Russia, the Exarch went to see his former professor of religion
at the Gymnasium of Petrograd, Father Constantine Smirnov,
who meanwhile had become Metropolitan of Kazan. He suggested to him a common course of action to be taken by
Orthodox and Catholics in the defense of religion. The
Metropolitan received him very cordially and called him by
his old nickname "Lionia," but showed little interest in the
project because he did not think that the Bolsheviks would
remain in power for any length of time. Actually, a few
months later the unfortunate Russian people would find
themselves carried back five thousand years to the time of the
Pharaohs. They would lose all those rights which Western
men, inspired by Christian respect for the individual, had so
laboriously vindicated through the centuries: the right to
freely seek objective truth; to follow their own consciences
and to worship accordingly; to own private property; to freely
establish contact with the rest of mankind by traveling, speaking, reading and writing as they wanted. Soviet Russia was to
become an immense labor camp where millions of slaves
would toil according to the whim of the new pharaohs, the
leaders of the Communist Party.

CHAPTER THIRTEEN

Visits to Patriarch Tikhon

THE passage to Catholicism of individual personages such as Miss Julia Danzas or the publicist Dimitri Kuzmine-Karavaiev, the union of entire parishes such as that of Father Potapii, offered a very limited solution to the imperious problem of Christian reconciliation. Certainly the Exarch warmly rejoiced in such conversions, for in addition to the spiritual benefit which the individuals enjoyed, they helped to awaken others who were indifferent to the problem of Reunion and, in addition, they heightened the prestige of the two model parishes which Father Leonid had established.

However, the Exarch aimed higher. He wanted Reunion to take place through the reconciliation of the hierarchies. This reconciliation was possible; he strongly believed it, but he seemed to be the only one who did. All the Catholic priests of the Latin rite had but one immediate goal: to attract as many Orthodox to their communities as they could by having them pass over to the Latin rite. "The opposition of the Catholics of the Latin rite to the embryos of parishes of Byzantine rite remains very strong," he wrote on many an oc-

casion, "above all in Moscow." Fortunately, the new Archbishop of Mohiliov, Mgr. John Tseplyak, was favorable to
his apostolate although his mentality remained that of a well-
disposed foreigner.

Three White Russian priests and a few Lithuanians generously supported the Exarch. The price of the least com-
modity was so high that, in order to exist, he had to request
material aid from his Latin brothers. "This is hard," he
confessed, "above all for the leader of a mission." [1] Another
very painful trial for him had been the long waiting period
before the Holy See confirmed the foundation of the Exarchate. This silence on the part of Rome allowed all who opposed
his views to contradict him at will or to smile at his efforts.
When finally, after waiting four years, the good news had
arrived,* he wrote on April 29, 1921: "The confirmation of
the Exarchate has produced a profound impression, and the
title of Apostolic Protonotary conferred on me by the Pope
came as a thunderbolt." [2]

Nevertheless, all the difficulties had not been eliminated.
On July 18, 1921, Father Leonid wrote a letter to Mgr.
Alexander Evreinov, a former Russian diplomat who had
become a priest in Rome. The regular mail abroad was not
functioning, and he sent three copies of this letter by different
travelers, hoping that at least one would reach its destination.
The Exarch begged the Russian prelate to send him, no
matter by what means, a copy of the *Acta Apostolicae Sedis*
(the official bulletin of the Vatican) which published the
confirmation of his appointment as Exarch. This document
was absolutely necessary in order to deal with some members
of the Latin clergy who continued to doubt his nomination.

In this letter he again emphasized the opposition he was
encountering. "The Poles," he wrote, "have spent centuries
in the midst of the Russians without ever understanding them

* See pp. 107–8.

or seeing all the spiritual values in their traditions. They regard their mission as not preaching in favor of Reunion but as the proselytism of isolated persons. They want to win over the people behind the back of the Orthodox clergy; they do not want to get close to the Orthodox clergy and moreover they would be incapable of doing so. A feeling of bitterness lies in the depths of their hearts after the suffering they formerly had to endure from those whom they call 'the cassocked police'; this feeling prevents them from acting with true apostolic kindness. As a result, in their meetings with Orthodox priests, they remain always on the defensive, never appear sincere and seem too evasive. This immediately becomes evident to the Orthodox priests who have a sharp, almost morbid sensitivity. Wanting to be an apostle yet keeping a heavy stone hidden beneath one's armpit is not an easy thing to do." Further on, he continues: "The Latin clergy is disconcerted by the passivity of our people who allow a band of rascals to profane its grandiose sanctuaries, and they draw the conclusion that the Russian people have lost the faith. Of course, by purely logical standards this conclusion carries weight, but in practice, this is not what is happening. Our people are formidable precisely because of their capacity for limitless endurance to put up with the blows of fate and for their obduracy. The Russian people will accept certain compromises with their conscience as the result of a kind of negligence; they do not consider this an apostasy. Naturally, this is not only a very difficult thing to grasp, but is impossible for a foreign Catholic to understand." [3]

The Exarch tried to counteract the conduct of the Latin clergy by his own way of acting. In his own words: "From the very beginning, no sooner was I named Exarch of the Russian Catholic Church than I sought every means of entering into relations with the Orthodox clergy. The Metropolitan of Petrograd, Mgr. Benjamin, and several priests who enjoyed great influence over the clergy and the people gradually became my good friends. In 1918 (within a year of my appointment) I entered into relations with Patriarch Tikhon himself who cordially received me. At the same period we formed a united front with the Orthodox to defend ourselves against the Bolshevik aggressions. In 1919 we made a joint protest. For the first time in Russian history, the names of Orthodox and Catholic prelates were signed to a Christian document drawn up against infernal forces. Moved with pity by the charity with which we treated them, the souls of our separated colleagues began to soften. It was they who suggested we meet in order to discuss the problems of reunion. In addition, we established (Orthodox and Catholics) a common plan for a course in apologetics and for conferences to combat atheist propaganda. The war against Poland scuttled our projects because during hostilities the government forbade any meeting which was not a Communist one. The Orthodox priests prepared to make a spiritual retreat under my direction.

"Up to this year [1922] the Latin clergy had taken no initiative in this domain: it had merely adopted an attitude which made my action more difficult. Archbishop Ropp was a father and a protector for me; he encouraged my efforts with an eye to an increasingly stronger alliance with the Orthodox clergy. Then suddenly the devil, like a lion ever in search of some victim to devour, aroused in the hearts of certain Latin priests a tempestuous zeal to convert those Christians who were separated from us. The initiator of this affair was a certain Father Paul Khodkiewicz. In a room adjoining the Church of St. Catherine he organized conferences where certain words were spoken which deeply wounded the Orthodox. There was no lack of audience for these conferences and in two years more than 120 persons requested to be received into the Catholic Church. The Latin priests did not understand, or did not want to understand, that this short-lived success and these few souls, including many women of Polish origin, meant nothing compared to the colossal problem of the reconciliation of 100 million Orthodox who live in our country." [4]

The Exarch realized that all his plans were about to be destroyed. From the numerical point of view, the Latin parishes were much more impressive than his own; it was impossible to make the Orthodox believe that they did not represent the Catholic Church. He insisted. "The Latins answer," he wrote, "that Reunion of the Churches is a foolish idea and a fantasy. It is useless [they say] to establish relations with the Orthodox clergy because all these priests are dishonest and corrupt. [They argue that] to bring the Catholic clergy closer to the Orthodox would mean exposing it to the danger of indifferentism and would weaken Catholic action. Once again the usual refrain is heard: 'Cultivated Russians have no use for the Eastern rite; they want the Latin rite. . . . Multiply conversions without dreaming about corporate Reunion!' " [5]

In order to change the orientation of these conferences, the Exarch decided to mold them somewhat by taking a more active part in them. He gave six conferences, but later admitted that this had been a bad calculation on his part: in the eyes of the Orthodox, he appeared to be associated with the propaganda conducted against them.

Father Deibner became more and more neurasthenic, and he showed it by his invectives against the Orthodox. One night he was so disrespectful to the saints of the Russian Church, whose worship would be approved several years later by the Catholic Church, that the Exarch decided to take sanction: he forbade him to speak in public.

In response to this campaign, the Orthodox in turn called their faithful to anti-Catholic conferences. The danger of

Roman propaganda was loudly denounced; the Exarch was accused of being a "Jesuit *in a riassa*" (in Eastern cassock). Father Feodorov went to Metropolitan Benjamin to try and put an end to these scandalous exchanges of accusation and invective. He suggested that henceforth only members of the clergy and some specialists be admitted to these reunions in order that they might be pursued in a truly charitable spirit. The Metropolitan refused indignantly. "You promise us Union!" he cried. "You want us to meet like brothers in Christ and all this time your Latin priests are causing havoc to our flock behind our back!" The Exarch returned home very much affected by this refusal to join in a project on which he was resolutely set and, according to a witness, he wept over it. This was the collapse of his plans for an indefinite period.

In Moscow, the dialogue between Orthodox and Catholics continued in a more serene atmosphere. In general, Father Leonid went every two months to the capital to lead a conference and to visit influential persons who were favorable to Reunion. On one occasion, at the request of the participants, he outlined with masterly clarity the Catholic doctrine on the primacy of the Bishop of Rome. This lecture and the lively but courteous exchange of views which followed it occupied no less than three and a half hours.

Patriarch Tikhon was kept informed of these meetings and approved them. The Exarch often visited him. "I was received by the Patriarch," he wrote on August 1, 1921, "and I complained about the ungracious words which the Orthodox clergy of Petrograd had spread about me. The Patriarch greeted me very courteously; he asked me to join him in a cup of tea with honey and promised to calm those in Petrograd who did not agree with us.

"Personally," the Exarch stated, "the Patriarch sincerely desires Reunion, but he can do nothing because he is powerless in the sense that he has been stripped of all authority.

More than once he has complained of this to his clergy and laymen. The Council of Moscow (1917) limited his powers to such a point that one could say of him: *'Il règne mais ne gouverne pas!!'* (He rules but he does not govern)." [6] Patriarch Tikhon's position, however, became even more and more difficult. On February 24, 1922, the Soviet daily *Izvestia* announced that the Central Committee of the Soviets had ordered the local Soviets to seize the sacred vessels and other valuable objects in the churches. These objects, they insisted, had to be sold in order to buy food to save the starving people. The Patriarch allowed the Soviets to take some discarded objects no longer used for sacred services, but he forbade them to remove the sacred vessels and even threatened to excommunicate those who might hand them over. The Soviets doubled their attacks against him, accusing him of conspiring against them and of being in contact with a group of Russian emigré bishops headed by the former Metropolitan of Kharkov and Kiev, Anthony Krapovitsky. These bishops had met at Karlovtzi in Serbia and proclaimed their loyalty to the Romanov dynasty.

In order to weaken the Russian Church even further, the Soviets supported groups of priests who had separated from the Patriarchal Church in order to found dissident sects—particularly one called the "Living Church." The most active leader of this group was a priest of Petrograd, Father Alexander Vvedensky. These schismatics from the Patriarchal Church demanded a democratic administration of the Church, the elevation to the episcopate of married priests, and the possibility of a second marriage for widowed priests. On May 16, 1922 Patriarch Tikhon was placed under arrest and forbidden to leave his residence.

Persuaded that the divisions between Christians were greatly weakening resistance to the Soviets, some militant Orthodox of Moscow made an effort to increase the Patriarch's prestige. In his honor they organized a demonstration of loyalty on the occasion of his monastic feastday which fell on June 15, the day the Byzantine Church celebrates the feast of St. Tikhon, Bishop of Amathus. It was decided that on this day a delegation from each parish of Moscow would express its good wishes to the Patriarch and, as a token of attachment, offer him a modest gift. These militant Orthodox thought that if the Catholics would agree to take part in this demonstration, their presence would create a greater effect and compensate somewhat for the schism of the Living Church. They approached Father Abrikosov and he accepted, believing that at such a tragic hour everything which could cement Christian unity was in conformity to Christ's wish.

At the appointed hour, a Catholic delegation went to the Troitzkoe Podvorie (Monastery of the Holy Trinity) where the Patriarch resided. This delegation consisted of Father Vladimir and two laymen, Nicholas Nicolaevitch Alexandrov, who was soon afterwards to be ordained priest, and Vladimir Vassilievitch Balachov. Other delegations sent by the Orthodox parishes of Moscow arrived at the same time and all were led into a huge reception room.

On entering, the Patriarch first approached the Catholics and embraced Father Abrikosov. Father Vladimir congratulated him on the occasion and expressed his joy at being able at such a serious moment to show his respect for the Shepherd of the Russian Church. He added: "The outer obstacles on the road to the rapprochement of Orthodox and Catholics have fallen. One can therefore hope that the work for the reconciliation of the Churches will now progress successfully. The Catholic Church is praying unceasingly for Reunion; she encourages the workers who are devoted themselves to this task." [7] Father Vladimir then recalled the initiatives taken in the West to heighten the prestige of the Christian East and to prepare the paths to Reunion. Finally, he presented the

Patriarch with Pope Benedict XV's Prayer for Unity translated into Russian and beautifully handwritten on fine paper.

The Patriarch thanked him, stating that he followed with interest and sympathy the efforts to reestablish Christian unity, that he prayed constantly for this intention and felt happy to know that he was able to contribute his share in this noble undertaking. He then added that he encouraged his clergy to collaborate with the Catholics. Turning from this general subject, he asked Father Abrikosov, "Did you confirm Kuzmine-Karavaiev?" "No," Father Vladimir replied, "we receive the Orthodox without new Confirmation." The Patriarch was alluding to a question contested between Latin and Eastern Catholics. The Latins held that the sacrament of Confirmation conferred by the Russian Church was not valid because for the sacramental anointing Orthodox priests did not use their thumbs but a small stick. Eastern Catholics, on the other hand, insisted that Christ, author of the sacraments, had allowed the Church a certain latitude in form. Had the Holy See "reconfirmed" the hundreds of thousands of Orthodox who at Brest-Litovsk in 1596 had accepted union with Rome? Evidently not. The Latin clergy's attitude in this regard deeply wounded the Orthodox and it was quite obvious that the Patriarch himself was not indifferent in the matter. At the close of the interview, the Patriarch again embraced Father Abrikosov, then greeted the other groups who had come to do him honor.

These meetings between Orthodox and Catholics did not please the Communists; they reproached the Orthodox who had taken part for a lack of patriotism. Three days after the reception of the Catholic delegation at the Patriarch's residence, some agents of the secret police (GPU) went to Father Vladimir's apartment to arrest him. The priest was absent, and they made a minute search of all the rooms. Finding nothing suspicious, they telephoned to their leader. They soon departed, but before doing so, they left word for Father Vladimir that once back in his apartment he was not to leave. Several hours later, Father Vladimir was brought to the police headquarters where he was questioned by a Chekist named Shpitzberg. Obviously, a spy had been present at the reception at Troitzkoe Podvorie, and the police thought that the Catholics had delivered a secret message from the Pope to Patriarch Tikhon. Fortunately, Father Abrikosov had with him the text of Pope Benedict's prayer which he had given the Patriarch; he showed it to the police officers and for a while the affair was forgotten.

It is understandable that in militant Orthodox circles the gesture of the Russian Catholics had created a sensation and brought real relief. The meetings had to be repeated and this time the Orthodox took the initiative in inviting the Catholics to some public discussions on Reunion. There were two meetings of this kind, presided over by Bishop Ilarion Troitzky, the Patriarch's auxiliary and righthand man. Exarch Leonid came from Petrograd to Moscow to speak at the second meeting. These meetings were unproductive, however, because it became evident that there were too many people attending and that there was too great a difference of intellectual level among them. On both occasions, some nagging and stubborn member of the audience prevented the principal speakers from treating the fundamental questions by engaging them in the discussion of secondary and irrelevant matters. At the first meeting the injustice of Latin Catholics toward the Easterners who had settled in North America was again recalled. The second time it was the news which had reached Moscow the day before concerning the establishment of a national Church separated from the Catholic Church in Czechoslovakia. This information served as a springboard for one of the audience to begin invectives against the Catholics. "When I left the room," the Exarch confessed with the suffering of an apostle frustrated in his zeal, "I felt that I was crossing through a crowd which for the most part was hostile to me." By common agreement the Orthodox and Catholic organizers decided that they would invite to the following meetings a more reduced and more homogeneous number of participants.

As it turned out, the Soviets prevented the organization of other meetings. For all true believers in Russia, the horizon was becoming more and more somber. In July the intrepid Metropolitan Benjamin of Leningrad, the loss of whose friendship the Exarch Leonid had felt so deeply, was shot with three of his aides. One detail was extremely painful. During the trial which preceded the execution, the priest Alexander Vvedensky, the animator of the so-called Living Church, came to testify against him. The same persecution was begun against the Catholics.

At the end of the summer, some thirty intellectuals whom the Government considered forever impervious to Communist ideology, received the order to leave the country. Among these were Professors Berdyayev, Bulgakov, Frank and Lossky. They were warned that if they recrossed the frontier they would be shot. Father Vladimir Abrikosov and the publicist Dimitri Kuzmine-Karavaiev were also expelled for having organized meetings with the Orthodox.

On September 25 Father Abrikosov bade farewell to the community of Dominican Sisters and to his parishioners in Moscow. The separation took place after they had all sung together the *moleben* for travelers. At about noon the next day, September 27, Father Vladimir arrived in Petrograd. Mgr. Tseplyak, the Latin Catholic Archbishop, detained him a long time in order to entrust him with different messages for the Holy See. The next day, September 28, after celebrating the Divine Liturgy, Father Vladimir spent the rest of the day with the Exarch.

The Exarch deeply regretted the loss of Father Abrikosov, his most precious aid, at such a serious moment. He consoled himself, however, with the thought that in Rome Father Vladimir would be able to represent the interests of the Russian Catholics and act somewhat as the Exarch's proxy. So much remained to be done to enlighten the Holy See regarding the situation of Christians in Russia, especially the possibilities of bringing Orthodox and Catholics closer! That evening the Exarch went with Father Abrikosov to the ship which was to take him and his companion, D. V. Kuzmine-Karavaiev, to Germany. They reached Berlin on October 2, and from there they went to Rome. A year later D. V. Kuzmine-Karavaiev was to enter the Greek Seminary on Via Babuino in Rome, despite his nearly forty years once more to become a student; he would be ordained a priest on July 3, 1927.

Soon after the exiles had left Russia, the Exarch received a letter from Father Onesimov, his priest in Saratov. "Bishop Freser, the Apostolic Vicar of the Latin rite, has arrived in Saratov," he wrote. "I have been to see him three times, but until now I was unable to convince him. He is obstinate and until now has refused to allow me to sing the Liturgy. He bases his refusal on the following reasons: 1) He has not seen the slightest document from Rome about our Eastern priests; 2) certain faithful of the Latin rite are already protesting because a priest of the Byzantine rite has been authorized to celebrate in private, without singing, in their church. If he authorizes me to celebrate, he insists, it will only be because he knows I am a good man." [8]

On October 30, 1922, the Exarch wrote a letter to Father Abrikosov in which he confirmed the recommendations he had made to him before his departure. "The main question —all others being secondary—" he wrote, "is to obtain from the Holy See a document addressed to the [Latin] dioceses of Mohiliov and Tiraspol to confirm to them that the Eastern Catholics have their hierarchy in Russia and are not vagrant gypsies." [9] In order to avoid any ambiguity, he strongly requested that his position be clearly defined. Metropolitan Andrew was disliked by the Russians; the Exarch therefore should no longer have to invoke the jurisdictional powers which he formerly had received from him. The Exarch's jurisdiction should come directly from Rome. He hoped, finally, that for once and all the Holy See would explicitly and insistently recommend the priests of the Byzantine rite to the Latin Ordinaries.

Father Abrikosov's reply was cruelly disappointing. He confessed that at Rome he received a cold reception. The Exarch had insisted that he have a private talk with the Holy Father, but he had been unable to do so. Fearing that Father Vladimir would be discouraged, the Exarch again took up his pen, and, in spite of the difficulty of getting a letter abroad he wrote him on December 13: "So you have received the first slap in the face! Congratulations! You know, it's a good sign. If everything at the beginning were easy, the rest might have been worse later on. When the Holy Father received you in the presence of others, you should immediately have requested a private audience. Without going into explanation, you should have told him that the Exarch had instructed you to communicate certain things orally. If people drive you away from the door, you must enter through the window. If they drive you away from the window, you must enter through a crack. Don't forget that Rome likes insistence and energy. If someone does not show this insistence, they think he is not convinced about his ideas." [10]

The coolness of Vatican authorities toward a priest who

had arrived from Moscow and could have given much vital
information about the situation in Russia was, of course, very
surprising. It gave rise to many comments. As Father Abrikosov himself reported later, the main reason for that attitude
was the following: the Vatican feared that by honoring too
ostensibly a priest whom the Soviets had exiled it would provoke further restrictions against the Catholics in Russia.

Prince Peter and Princess Marie Volkonsky, who were
staying in Rome at that time, wrote to the Exarch that Reverend Father Vladimir Ledochowski, the Jesuit General, although of Polish nationality, showed a sincere interest in
Father Vladimir's actions and that one could rely on him.
Through the intermediary of Father Edmund Walsh, the
Exarch at once wrote and asked him to support Father Abrikosov at Rome. "He is a man of God," he wrote, "a sincere,
learned and prudent Catholic, a man of high moral values,
a true confessor of the faith, for he was twice imprisoned by
the Bolsheviks for a period of seven months. . . ."

The Exarch took advantage of that letter to announce
the coming storm. "The Catholic Church in Russia is undergoing a terrible crisis," he wrote. "The government is trying
to impose on us a concordat, whereby in every parish the
power would be given to laymen and the priest would become
an employee. In spite of all my protests, every Catholic
church in Petrograd has been closed by force because we have
refused to sign this concordat. . . . I am now in Moscow
and tomorrow or the next day I will go with Father Budkiewicz, pastor of the Church of St. Catherine, to protest to the
Central Government against this act of violence, but—
humanly speaking—I have hardly any hope of success."

Next the Exarch explained to Father Ledochowski that
even priests were forbidden to teach religion to those under
eighteen or to allow them to sing in the church choirs. Atheism was officially taught in the schools. After having divulged

that the police had threatened him with arrest, he added: "For my part, I'm ready for anything and I have already prepared my faithful of Petrograd and Moscow for any eventuality. The government has threatened either to deport me or to have me shot. May the will of God be done." [11] The Exarch was not mistaken: the crisis occurred a few hours later.

CHAPTER FOURTEEN

Arrest—the Moscow Trial

AT the end of 1922 no one in ecclesiastical circles in Russia
had any doubt that a violent religious persecution was about
to begin. The Soviet government had shown clearly that it
intended to strip the churches of their sacred vessels and other
precious objects. This meant that everything possible must be
done to prevent places of worship from being profaned. For
this reason, and because they expected churches to be closed,
at least for a time, the Catholic parishes had carefully chosen
safe hiding-places for chalices and everything else that was
needed to celebrate the sacred rites in case they were forced
to do so outside the churches.

"In Barmalayeva Street," Miss Danzas tells us, "only what
was strictly necessary was left behind in the church. The rest
was hidden partly in Mrs. Deibner's house and partly in mine.
It seemed likely that if there was a search they would go first
to Father Feodorov's apartment and then to Mrs. Deibner's,
because it was close to the church; so the safest place seemed
to be the little apartment which I occupied above Father

Feodorov, and it was there that we set up a small altar and everything else that we would need . . . " [1]

The last solemn Liturgy was celebrated in the church in Barmalayeva Street on November 21, 1922, the feast of the Presentation of the Virgin. The following day after the Liturgy, which was celebrated at seven o'clock in the morning and without particular ceremony, the police came to arrest the Exarch. This is how Miss Danzas tells the story: "I had gone back home for a few minutes, and at eight o'clock I was going as usual to my work at the Public Library, when I saw Father Feodorov at the corner of the street between two soldiers who were taking him to the local police station. I managed to get in front of them by taking a short cut, so that I found myself approaching Father Feodorov. When he saw me he glanced toward the church and murmured, as if he were talking to himself: *"Sanctissimum."* His guards took no notice. However Miss Danzas immediately understood that the Exarch was afraid the police would profane the Holy Eucharist which was kept in a little ciborium on the altar.

There was no time to be lost; she went to the church, made the usual prostration before the altar, and took off the silk cloth which covered the small lectern beside the altar; then she opened the tabernacle, took out the little casket containing the Blessed Sacrament, and placed it in the antimension. Finally she rolled the antimension in the silk cloth, and hiding it under her coat she left the church by a door concealed behind a cupboard. She was not seen by the police and they did not notice the door through which she left.

At the police station the interrogation was quite short. The Exarch was given provisional freedom but told not to leave the city, and the police sealed up the doors of the church.

After wandering through the surrounding streets for some time, considering to what other Catholic church she could take the Host, Miss Danzas decided to go first to see what was happening in the Exarch's apartment. He had just been released, and, meeting Miss Danzas in the courtyard of the apartment building, he went home, consumed the Host and remained for a long time in prayer.

The police had not sealed the second door to the church which had escaped their notice, but it was not possible to go on holding services there. Miss Danzas therefore offered the parish her drawing-room, and a little altar was put up in it and hidden by a screen when services were finished. The first few days after these events, the Holy Liturgy was celebrated as unobtrusively as possible and in the presence of only a small congregation. On Christmas Eve 1922, they risked singing the evening office with subdued voices; there were no incidents. After this they decided to sing the Sunday and holy-day services in the same way. Unfortunately they were denounced by a neighbor, and on January 6, the feast of the baptism of Our Lord according to the calendar of the Eastern Church, the faithful had just taken Communion and the Exarch was finishing the Divine Liturgy when there was an unusually loud ring at the door. They realized at once that it must be the police. Miss Danzas opened the door and four policemen came in.

"What is going on here?" they asked.

It was impossible to disguise the truth. The incense, the candles, the icons and the priest in vestments all showed clearly what was taking place.

"We are praying, comrades." Miss Danzas replied.

"What do you mean?"

"But everything is in order: we are not breaking the law. There are less than twenty people here, and there are no minors among us." [2]

The policemen wandered around the apartment for a few minutes and then left, muttering against "popish trickery."

Services were held for a few weeks after this in an atmosphere and seclusion like that of the catacombs. Those who were present never forgot them. In the evening, before going home, Father Feodorov liked to kneel in front of the little makeshift altar, and he would often stay there in prayer for several hours on end. "When I feel overwhelmed by misfortune," he once said, "the greatest joy that the Lord can give me is to go to the altar, to put my forehead against it (as on the day of my ordination to the priesthood), and to feel the presence of the only reality. Not only does calm return, but my body seems to be annihilated; the only true life begins, the life of that which is intangible." [3]

Throughout this period the Latin Ordinary, Archbishop Tseplyak, had continued to negotiate with the Soviet government concerning the property of the Catholic Church. The Soviets demanded that in future this property should be managed entirely by committees of laymen under the control of the state. The Holy See refused, and the Archbishop was forced to try to find a compromise. Without waiting for this, the Soviets had closed and sealed off Catholic churches of Latin rite in Petrograd, and the faithful in the city were not able to use them for the Christmas celebration in the year 1922.

A month later, that is to say early in February 1923, Archbishop Tseplyak, Exarch Feodorov, and thirteen priests of Catholic parishes in Petrograd were ordered to go to Moscow to appear before the Revolutionary High Court. They were accused of offenses against a number of Soviet laws. Father Feodorov in particular was charged with resisting the decree that churches should be stripped of their sacred vessels, of having had criminal contacts with foreign countries, of teaching religion to minors, and finally of having spread antirevolutionary propaganda. Some of the priests were also charged with spying for a foreign power (Poland).

The police decided that this time they would avoid making

spectacular arrests. The priests were ordered to leave together on the same evening and to buy their tickets themselves; two compartments in the same train were reserved for them.

They set out on the night of the second to the third of March. All the Catholics in Petersburg who could came to the station to say good-by to their pastors. It was an imposing and deeply moving scene. Archbishop Tseplyak had told his priests to insist that the faithful avoid any demonstration which might provoke disorder and bring about the intervention of the armed police who surrounded the station platform. The Poles have always been courageous and attached to their priests, and as they were well in the majority in this large and indignant crowd, a spark would have been enough to start a disturbance which would have caused a clash with the police, but the Archbishop's orders were dutifully obeyed. When the train began to move, Archbishop Tseplyak and the other priests standing at the windows blessed their parishioners, and the crowd, which had stood in silence on the platform until that moment, began to chant the *Sub tuum praesidium*—"We place ourselves in thy hands, O Virgin Mary." The singing continued until the lights of the train had vanished into the darkness of the night.

The priests did not arrive in Moscow until two days later, on March 5. Those of Polish origin were permitted to stay in the presbytery of the Latin Church of Sts. Peter and Paul; the Exarch stayed with some friends. On Saturday March 10, at 6.30, the Archbishop and his priests were taking their evening meal when the presbytery was encircled by troops; they were put into an open truck, surrounded by soldiers, and as a further insult, driven through the main thoroughfares of Moscow to a government building at No. 6 Pretchistensky Boulevard. At midnight the same night the Exarch was also arrested and brought to join the Latin priests. They were kept in two rooms in the building and obliged to sleep either on chairs or on the floor. Two days later, at 2.30 in the

afternoon, they were again driven across the city and transferred to the Butyrka prison. Father Edmund Walsh followed
their movements and managed each time to get some food
to them from the Pontifical Mission which was still fully
active in Russia.

As soon as the Holy See was informed of the arrest of the
Archbishop and his priests, Cardinal Gasparri, Secretary of
State, made an urgent appeal to Mr. Vorovsky, head of the
Soviet mission in Rome, but he could get no more than an
assurance that the lives of the accused were not in danger.
The Anglican Archbishop of Canterbury, the Lutheran
Swedish Bishop of Upsala, Cardinal Mercier of Malines—one
of the most widely respected figures in Europe at the time—
and numerous government intervened in their turn, but
could obtain no more positive result.

The trial began on March 21 and lasted five days. The
sessions were held in the ballroom of the former Nobles'
Club, called the Blue Room because of the color of its walls.
Father Walsh followed all of them with the help of a Russian
stenographer.[4] Large notices reading 'Positively No Smoking'
hung around the walls of the hall, but this did not stop
Prosecutor Krylenko and the three judges from smoking continuously. There were sixteen prisoners: Archbishop Tseplyak, Exarch Leonid, thirteen priests and one layman.
Among the priests was Monsignor Constantine Budkiewicz,
the pastor of St. Catherine's Catholic Church in Petrograd,
who was also a canon of Mohiliov and a member of the administrative council of the Mohiliov diocese. There was no
jury; the sentence was to be pronounced by the three judges,
all three Communists. The first, named Galkin, was an apos-
tate priest; the second was a worker, and the third a peasant.
Sixteen soldiers, one for each of the accused men, stood
guard over them with fixed bayonets.

An Englishman, Captain Francis McCullagh, was present

throughout the trial as a journalist. He notes that in many ways Exarch Leonid was the "most picturesque figure in the court. A handsome, well-built man in the prime of life, with that strong, gentle, Christlike face which is so often found among Russian peasants, with long dark hair, a noble beard, and the ample, flowing robes of a Russian ecclesiastic, he formed a striking contrast to the shaven Roman priests with their close-fitting soutanes and close-cropped hair. Although he confessed that he was the son of a Petrograd cook and the grandson of a serf, his manner was as dignified as if he had been born to the purple, and, as we shall soon see, his words were more than worthy of his manner."

There were three charges against the prisoners: they had given religious instruction to children; they had refused to hand over the property of the Church; and they had continued to hold services after the churches had been closed. The reading of the indictment lasted exactly an hour.

From the beginning Prosecutor Krylenko, an ardent Communist, was unable to disguise his hatred. "You love your religion," he said to the prisoners sarcastically, "Well then, carry your cross . . ." And later: "I spit on your religion, as I spit on all religions: Orthodox, Jewish, Muslim, Lutheran and the rest. Yes, as Feodorov has said, with all the subtlety of a Jesuit, we give civil recognition to football clubs, but we refuse it to the Church. . . ."

At the start of the second day the Exarch was attacked by Krylenko for not surrendering church property to the government.

Krylenko to the Exarch: "You refused to sign the agreement to hand over the property of the Church to the government?"

Feodorov: "Yes."

Krylenko: "You consider that you are not obliged to obey the laws?"

Feodorov: "I obey Soviet laws as long as they are not against my conscience."

Krylenko (angrily): "Leave your conscience out of it! I am asking you a simple question: do you obey the Soviet government or not?"

Feodorov: "If the Soviet government asks me to act against my conscience I do not obey it. Insofar as teaching the catechism is concerned, the doctrine of the Catholic Church is that children must receive religious instruction whatever the law says. One's conscience is above the law. No law which goes against one's conscience is binding."

Krylenko: "Ah!"

Judge Galkin (angrily): "We do not want to hear any more about your conscience. Your conscience does not interest us."

Feodorov: "Well, I personally am very interested in it."

After questioning the other priests on the same point, Krylenko came back to the charge: "Feodorov, you celebrated the liturgy after the closing of the churches."

Feodorov: "Yes."

Krylenko: "Where?"

Feodorov: "In an apartment of the house where I live."

Krylenko: "How many people were present?"

Feodorov: "From 20 to 25."

The cross-examination of Archbishop Tseplyak only began on the second day, at 11.00 p.m. This detail alone is enough to show the sort of man Prosecutor Krylenko was: at eleven at night he began to question a venerable churchman worn with age—he was nearly seventy—already exhausted by two days of continual strain.

On the third day the Prosecutor once more questioned the Exarch alone, and asked him about his origins, where he had studied, and the different rites of the Catholic Church. In particular he accused him of having written a pamphlet on *The Separation of Church and State in Bolshevik Russia* in collaboration with an Orthodox priest, Father Kuznetzov, who was later to be condemned and shot. The Exarch agreed that he had written the pamphlet, and added: "As far as organizing committees of Orthodox Christians in conjunction with Catholics is concerned, I took the matter as far as I could, but if I failed, I don't know why . . ."

On the fourth day in a long interrogation Comrade Krylenko again questioned the Exarch separately. "Let us return to the case of Comrade Feodorov," he said. "He is a remarkable man. His human qualities make him comparable to Comrade Budkiewicz, but he is far superior to him in his attitude and in his intelligence. Budkiewicz behaves like a Jesuit, calculating and shrewd. But Feodorov is straightforward in his dealings; and these dealings should not be explained by simple fanaticism. He was the one who organized the reunions with the Orthodox clergy. He was the one who worked out the plan to combine all these counter-revolutionary organizations to defeat Soviet laws. As a preventive measure he must be deprived of the power to do harm. He should be judged not only for what he has done but for what he is capable of doing."

At the end of his speech Krylenko asked for the death penalty for the two most prominent ecclesiastics, Archbishop Tseplyak and Monsignor Budkiewicz, as an example to others. His last words were greeted with loud applause by the crowd. When his speech was finished, during the pleas of the defense lawyers, Judge Galkin settled down to read a novel.

There were two lawyers defending the priests of Latin rite, but the Exarch chose to conduct his own defense. He began by declaring: "My whole life has been based on two foundations: love of the Church to which I have united myself, and love of my country which is dear to me. I do not mind whether I am condemned to ten years' imprisonment, or to be shot, but this is not because I am a fanatic. Since I gave myself to the Catholic Church, my chief idea has been to reconcile my country with it, because I believe it to be the one true Church. The government has not understood us. . . . If everything we have said in our meetings and our discussions was known, we would not be here, accused of having held secret meetings. That accusation is utterly without foundation. If we opposed the decrees which disposed of Church property without any consideration for the religious consciences of Catholics, it was not at all through concern for ourselves, but solely because of the laws of the Church. For us the canons of the Church are absolutely sacred things. The supreme pastoral authority of the Roman Pontiff is a dogma of our Catholic faith, and submission to the man whom we consider to be the representative of Jesus Christ on earth is a strict obligation for us. So it is a question of principle for us, and not of disobeying the law for our own material interests."

The Exarch went on to describe how at first he had welcomed the separation of the Church and the State, hoping that it would give more freedom to Catholics, and how he had later been disillusioned on this point. Then he turned to the question of teaching the catechism to children. "What would the Church be if she did not teach? If, for example, young people of between sixteen and eighteen come to me to be married, how can I prepare them for marriage without explaining certain religious ideas to them? And you—don't you yourselves teach young people of less than eighteen? What would a child be like if he had learned nothing before the age of eighteen?"

The President: "You are criticizing the laws of the Soviet government."

Feodorov: "I am simply explaining my religious beliefs. According to the Constitution, I can preach my religious ideas. Why can I not preach them to children?"

The President: "It is forbidden by the law! You are not explaining your religious beliefs, you are putting forward reasoned arguments . . ."

Feodorov: "I cannot help giving reasons. I cannot take my heart in my hands and show it to you! . . . If we really have freedom of worship, you cannot burn us at the stake."

The President stopped him, but he continued: "Well then, let me explain to you the condition of our souls in another way. Our faith is the sole force behind our religious life and it drives us to convert other men. If Communists were forbidden to teach Communist principles to their children before they reached the age of eighteen, would they obey such an order? Then why does the law deprive us of the right to hand on our religious faith to our children? All publications dealing with these subjects have been forbidden in Russia."

The President: "Have you tried to obtain them from abroad?"

Feodorov: "Yes. Philosophical books have been allowed in, but books of theology were confiscated on the frontier."

The President: "You should have mentioned this at the preliminary hearing and you could have lodged a complaint. Now it is too late."

Feodorov: "Let me finish. The objections which we have made against the government were not of a revolutionary nature. I would like to emphasize this. The property of my church was confiscated without us putting up any resistance. We are accused of not wanting to give up the property of the Church so that it can be used for the noble purpose of saving people from starvation. Let me remind you that forty trucks of food were sent by Pope Benedict XV and that one hundred and twenty thousand children are being fed at the moment by Pope Pius XI."

The President: "What has that to do with it? Even though

the Pope helps the starving, Catholics can still defy the laws. We are interested in your own case and not in other people's affairs."

Feodorov: "I am coming to that."

The President: "It's about time you did."

Feodorov: "I have never concealed anything. The government knew everything, and it cannot accuse me of belonging to secret organizations. All these misunderstandings can be explained by the contradictory orders which we received from the government. We did not know what to do. We are not guilty either of counterrevolution or of forming a secret organization, and still less of trying to resist the Soviet government or of wanting to overthrow it. That is all I have to say . . ."

In his plea one of the lawyers for the Polish priests, Mr. Borishchev-Pushkin, had suggested that they should simply all be expelled from Russia. Krylenko rejected this proposal. "What would this deportation abroad mean?" he asked. "It would simply be throwing the fish back into the water. We ought to punish them in such a way that no one will wish to copy them."

The Exarch was offered a last chance to speak in his own defense. "I have nothing more to say," he declared. "Our hearts are full not of hatred but of sadness. You cannot understand us. You do not give us freedom of conscience. That is the only conclusion that I can draw from what I have heard here."

The President: "Is that your conclusion?"

Feodorov: "It is, and it is also very painful to me. That is all I can say."

Captain Francis McCullagh thought that the Exarch's speech in itself threw more light on the contradictions and injustices of the Bolsheviks who were trying them than did the pleas of the other lawyers. He showed skilfully how the whole trial was simply a performance and its outcome determined from the start. But he did this without bitterness, as a man whose position was so strong that he had no need to defend himself, or as a pastor less concerned with saving his own life than with preventing his persecutors from committing what was clearly an injustice.

During the trial he emphasized that he was not under the jurisdiction of any Polish bishop of the Latin rite, but of Metropolitan Sheptitzky of Lvov, who was in fact in difficulties with the Polish government at the time and had been kept in prison. Thus he showed how unfair it was to accuse him of working for Poland.

At one point during the trial one of the Latin priests almost fainted with fatigue. A man in obviously poor health, he seemed unable to follow what was being said, and when he was cross-examined by Krylenko he simply answered, even to unimportant questions: "I am a Catholic priest." Then there was a short adjournment. When the prisoners came back to the stand, this priest was seen to take a different place from the one he had occupied until then. He sat between the Exarch and the youngest of the accused, Father Edward Yunevich, a man from Bielorussia, and he stayed there until the end of the trial. Evidently the Exarch and his young colleague had put him back on his feet and he had regained his strength; when he was questioned again he spoke with as much clarity and force as the others.

On the last day the prisoners were once again allowed to speak briefly in their defense. The Exarch was the last to do so: "I cannot do better," he said, "than to stress that I agree with what Archbishop Tseplyak has said. Like him I had to consider my office and give a good example to my subordinates. I have never done anything in secret. Everything I did was known to the government. No one among the authorities can point to anything counterrevolutionary in what

I have done. I simply ask the judges to consider the words of my colleague, Father Edward Yunevich. They were the cry of a tortured soul, the soul of a Catholic priest summoned before you, and this cry finds an echo in the souls of each one of us. . . . I simply ask the judges to weigh and consider the situation which forced this cry from the soul of a Catholic priest. It is due to the fact that the sacred duty which we have to fulfill as priests is in conflict with what is prescribed by the civil law. We are the victims of misunderstanding, and I do not see how we can escape from this. If the Almighty will accept our sacrifice on this Palm Sunday, if some good seed may spring from our bodily suffering, to grow and ripen, to be accepted and appreciated by our dear fatherland which I love so deeply, I wish only that through this experience, however painful it may be, our fatherland may come to realize that the Christian faith and the Catholic Church are not political organizations but a community of love. In this I see the providence of God, the will of God, and believing this I am prepared to accept whatever He sends."

The judges let the prisoners wait for eight hours, and then they came back, arranging the time of their return to the court so that the sentences were read exactly at midnight. The Exarch was sentenced to ten years imprisonment. Archbishop Tseplyak and Mgr. Budkiewicz were condemned to be shot. The other priests were given sentences ranging from three to ten years imprisonment. All their possessions were confiscated.

Archbishop Tseplyak and Mgr. Budkiewicz appealed to the Supreme Praesidium: Mgr. Budkiewicz's appeal was rejected and he was executed. Details gathered from various sources lead us to believe that as he came out of his cell he was shot from behind with a revolver bullet in the head. Archbishop Tseplyak's sentence was commuted to ten years of solitary confinement.

Once this parody of a trial was over, the prisoners were piled into a completely closed truck, without windows, and taken back to the Butyrka prison. It was ten minutes past one in the morning.

CHAPTER FIFTEEN

The Prisons of Moscow

SINCE six o'clock in the evening, an automobile had been waiting before the door of the tribunal: it was that of Father Walsh. As soon as the trial had ended, the Jesuit, who had followed it with the aid of a stenographer, jumped into his automobile, returned to the headquarters of the Pontifical Mission and, at two o'clock in the morning, telegraphed to Rome in a roundabout way the sentence which had been passed on the priests. This had not been easy; government censorship had blocked every telegram of press agency representatives. However, a telegraph line, that of the British Commercial Office, had been left open. Father Walsh obtained their cooperation; it is likely that the English that night thus saved the life of Archbishop Tseplyak. In fact, protests arrived from every corner of the world, especially from the Great Powers: Germany, Brazil, the United States and France. In the name of the Italian people, Mussolini himself intervened.

At two-thirty in the morning, Father Walsh began to take steps to obtain an audience with the Minister of Foreign Affairs, Chicherin, but this was finally refused. Together with his aides, the Father spent the rest of the night in translating the principal passages of the trial recorded in shorthand. He sent them abroad and they were published in several newspapers, especially the *New York Herald* and the *Civiltà Cattolica.*[1]

The indignation which this trial caused outside Russia seemed to have produced a certain impression on the government. The prisoners were moved to the Sokolniki prison and for the first months were submitted to a relatively easy régime. Only Archbishop Tseplyak was isolated. Father Walsh was permitted but one brief visit to him after promising that he would not speak in Latin to the prelate, and guards were present during this conversation.

The other priests remained together. There was sufficient food; moreover, Father Walsh did not forget them. Visits were permitted. In theory, they could not last longer than fifteen minutes, but it was easy for a visitor to put the guard in an excellent mood by slipping five or six rubles into his pocket. Thus the meeting was prolonged; friends could approach the bars, exchange letters with the prisoners, hand them parcels and whisper a few words. The guard noticed nothing; the rubles had a magic effect.

The Exarch's friends took advantage of this. They brought him books, writing paper and ink, and enabled him to profit by the long days of confinement which had been imposed on him. Father Leonid was thus able to draft two Catholic catechisms in Russian. In a letter he wrote: "I have begun to draw up a theological course in Russian based on Hurter, for I have realized that 95% of the Russian priests read nothing but Russian."[2] Miss Danzas made the trip from Petrograd to Moscow four times in order to visit him. "I can attest," she wrote, "that his attitude was calmer and more joyous than usual. He told me that he never felt so happy. He went so far as to accuse himself of selfishness because, he claimed, he enjoyed too much this calm after so many worries. He endured his imprisonment with the utmost serenity and assured me that it was not so bad as people thought." [3]

Obviously he spoke this way to prevent his friends from worrying about him. However, in a letter written at that time he confessed that one of his priest-companions had lost his mind and another had returned to childhood. "I have the greatest pity for my friend Father Yunevich," he wrote. "He endures his confinement courageously, and yet sometimes his nerves give way, but God's grace sustains him and prevents him from showing the slightest lack of courage." He added, "We soon hope to celebrate the holy Eucharistic Sacrifice. Thus our fate will be lightened; it will grant us new strength."

From a note he received he learned that Metropolitan Sheptitzky was still thinking of conferring the episcopal consecration upon him as soon as possible. The Exarch wrote him from prison on July 1, 1923 to dissuade him. "I don't belong," he assured him, "to that class of subjects known as 'hypocritically humble' who, after having protested with tears and cries of their unworthiness, nevertheless lower their heads beneath the omophorion [brocade band worn by the bishops of the Byzantine rite].* I have a healthy and realistic judgment which forces me to weigh every question seriously, above all those which concern the Church. If I am a good preacher, if I know every detail of the life of the Eastern Church, if I am able to celebrate the offices and even have a refined sense of our rite, if I am patient as a mule and know how to yield to all circumstances, if sometimes I give proof of great energy in defending the Church and spare neither my strength nor my health—all that does not entitle me to the episcopate. Any priest could accomplish all this successfully. People have spoken of my charity and skillful-

* Corresponds to the Western pallium.

ness; they have pointed out my capacity to penetrate human souls. But all these are merely the result of persistent efforts; they are virtues that come through necessity; they are not efforts which have come to me naturally and can never be identified with my real self. All this is merely a mask fastened to my face for a certain time while I await the complete man to whom I will be able to hand over this heavy load with a sigh of relief.

"I have examined myself severely and have come to the conclusion that someone built to climb should not attempt to fly. . . . I am incapable of working in a personal and independent way. Perhaps I have accomplished in an ideal manner the orders of others, but I am not a creator. I am not a Jacob wrestling with God, but a Job lying on his dung-hill. I have assimilated Western thought and its clarity, but, in fact, I am solidly rooted in the passive Eastern nature and remain rebellious to any action. The book, the cell, presence at the altar and at lengthy church ceremonies, and above all solitude and withdrawal from the world—this is the atmosphere which suits me; it is there that I feel like a fish in the water.

"I cannot lead an active and contemplative life at the same time. You know how much I love the Jesuits, but I would never decide to enter their Society, for their ideal (to unite contemplation with action) is not within my means. The most difficult thing for me is the society of men. I love them solely because the Lord wishes it so, or more precisely I endeavor to love them, but my heart remains a stranger to them. During the painful years (which I have endured), when from time to time I was broken down and exhausted, instead of resting I remained seated in an armchair for two or three hours, my only light being a small vigil lamp before the icon in a corner of my room, and I enjoyed my solitude. I became aware of the fact that I was completely cut off from the world; I thought of almost nothing and fixed my gaze on the face of Christ [the icon] illuminated by the soft light of the vigil lamp." [4]

The love of solitude did not prevent the Exarch from active preoccupation with the Catholic communities and the fate of the Russian Church. In spite of the barriers to cross, he conducted a large correspondence from his prison cell.

He thought above all of his faithful. On May 8, he wrote to Father Walsh: "The profound interest, the generous and unselfish care which you have shown toward the cause of the Catholic Church in Russia, increase in my heart the strongest friendship for you. Although entirely separated from my flock, I can enjoy peace, because I know that in you it has a noble defender and a protector who will not stop at any effort to aid our Catholic Church which is certainly very small but authentically Russian. . . . Only three priests remain attached to our Church in order to work in the Lord's vineyard: Father E.A., who is at Petrograd, Father Alexis Onesimov at Saratov and at Moscow Father Nicholas Alexandrov, whom you know quite well. I confide these three priests to you, knowing that in your zeal for the glory of God you will not refuse them your aid which will be as necessary as your advice." [5]

"At Sokolniki," he writes, "there are two [Orthodox] bishops and about twenty [Orthodox] priests. Our relations with them are the very best. I have schooled my Latin [companions] properly and never does a bitter word pass from their lips. I go continually to see them on the first floor and they receive me each time as one of their own. The Bishop, Boris R., seems especially well disposed towards Reunion. I think that I will be able to sow more than one handful of good seed.

"A rumor is going around that we will be sent to Rome. If we may hope for an amnesty (on May 1 or October 25th) *

---

* Labor Day and the anniversary of the Bolshevik Revolution.

which would reduce my term of prison to only two years, I would prefer to stay in prison those two years in order to be able to remain in Russia. Because even in prison I am able to do some good and even to administer the Exarchate. . . . Our communities have to lead a life of the catacombs. I have ordered them to meet in small groups and to recite prayers together in a low voice and to organize *besedi* (conferences). I have instructed them to teach parents the more advanced catechism, so that later they can teach their children since this is now forbidden to the priests. . . ." [6]

During the year 1923, Father Walsh took advantage of his presence in Moscow and of the authority he enjoyed as head of the Pontifical Mission of aid to the starving Russians to attempt to obtain from the government a *modus vivendi* acceptable for the Catholic parishes. In 1917, during the Revolution, Russia numbered 896 Catholic priests. In 1923, 60% of these priests were already either in prison or had been deported or forced to flee abroad, and the situation therefore became very serious. However, these negotiations failed.

Father Feodorov had followed them with a certain anguish, fearing that the Church might let herself be deceived. On July 22 he again wrote to Father Walsh: "We all learned with great joy the immutable decision of the Holy See not to make any further concession on the question of disciplinary and ecclesiastical order. That means that the Holy See now has a clear conception of the Bolsheviks. We are all deeply grateful to the Holy Father for his kindness which was so evident in his allocution on the Day of Pentecost. No imprisonment seems painful to us, for we have long been ready to shed our blood for Our Lord Jesus Christ. We have translated into Russian and Polish the words of the Holy Father in which he speaks of Russia and we are sending them everywhere. The [Holy Father's] loving and compassionate sentiments in regard to the Orthodox clergy impresses them profoundly. We Russian Catholics have long desired that the Holy Father should speak in this way to our separated brothers. These few lines dictated by the heart are worth the encyclicals of Benedict XV and Leo XIII." [7]

In such a tense atmosphere, it was not surprising that certain Catholic priests of the Latin rite who were still at liberty did not approve of Father Walsh. The echoes of these criticisms of him penetrated to the Sokolniki prison. The Exarch immediately took up his pen to defend his benefactor.

From his cell he wrote again on May 27 to the Reverend Father Ledochowski, the Jesuit General. He reiterated his esteem for Father Walsh and continued: "I would be so happy if your Paternity would tell me the accusations brought to Rome against Father Walsh. As an eye witness, I could make certain declarations." Then, with his usual frankness, he added: "Be kind enough, however, to write rather clearly, for it is sometimes difficult to decipher your letters." A prisoner in his position naturally found it frustrating not to be able to read the letters he received.[8] He also wrote a short letter to Father Abrikosov and ended with these words: "Ask God to help me better to endure the privation of the Holy Eucharist." [9] He pressed him with questions on the Church's action in favor of Russia and of those Russians who had emigrated; he finally insisted that the Father make known his prayer for Christian Unity.

During his confinement he also took the greatest interest in following the trials which the Patriarchal Russian Church was undergoing. On April 29, 1923, the schismatic group which had taken the name of the "Living Church" opened a Sobor which they wanted to consider as a second Pan-Russian Council following that of 1917. Patriarch Tikhon was still in prison; he was about to be tried and many feared that the death penalty would be imposed. Most of the parishes of the large cities had left him to join the Living Church. The Sobor declared the Patriarchate abolished and the Patriarch reduced to the layman's state. Then suddenly, on June 25, the sensational news spread everywhere that Patriarch Tikhon had been liberated. It was soon learned that on June 15 he had published a declaration to the Supreme Court which ended with these words: "I declare that henceforth I will no longer be an enemy of the Soviet power. Finally and in a decisive manner, I withdraw from the monarchist counterrevolutionary movement of the White Guards either abroad or in Russia herself."

Immediately many parishes which had left the Patriarchal Church for the Living Church made an about-face, and proclaimed their fidelity to the Patriarch. "The Tikhonian Church is triumphing daily on every front," the Exarch wrote at that time with obvious joy. "The Orthodox Church is again showing its inexhaustible vitality and its infinite capacity for adaptation. It is again emerging almost intact from a terrible danger. The authority of the Russian Orthodox clergy is increasing and acquiring more and more influence. In the eyes of the Russian people, it appears unfortunate and persecuted. Its popes * have become martyrs. The past is forgiven and forgotten. The clergy's word has acquired a great deal of weight and influence." [10]

Unfortunately, the Catholic priests did not remain longer than five months at the Sokolniki prison. In mid-September, the Exarch was suddenly transferred to the Lefort prison. It was beyond the city and its regime was stricter; in fact, it had the reputation of being the strictest of all Moscow. Miss Danzas managed to see the Exarch only once and for only five minutes. Two bars separated her from the prisoner. Between

* The Russian priests.

the two walked a stern guard. Before leaving, she wanted to ask the Exarch's blessing, but the jailer became angry and pitilessly drove her away.

Thus months went by for the prisoners, living in complete isolation and depressed by the silence and monotony. Fortunately, the Exarch had learned to live with God alone in utter solitude. On rare occasions some outside news managed to reach the prisoners: on January 21, 1924, Lenin died and a few days later on January 26, the city of Petrograd changed its name to Leningrad. The struggle between Stalin, the new dictator, and Trotsky, as well as with Lenin's old comrades, was reaching its height. On April 7, 1925, Patriarch Tikhon died. For fifteen years his patriarchal chair was to remain without a titulary.

It is not certain that in his seclusion the Exarch had learned of the sad fate reserved for the rest of his friends. In November 1923, Mother Abrikosov and all her spiritual daughters were arrested in Moscow at the same time as Miss Danzas and other Catholics of Petrograd and all were sent to prison. It seems that these arrests had been provoked by unforgivable imprudence. A letter written by Miss Danzas containing information about the religious persecutions and sent outside Russia by a roundabout way was naïvely published under her name in a Western European review. Of the three Catholic priests of Petrograd, Father Zerchaninov, despite his seventy-five years, was sent to Siberia with a young Russian priest ordained by Archbishop Tseplyak shortly before his arrest; Father Deibner, who was already ill, was kept in painful isolation in a Vladimir prison where he suffered above all from lack of food.

Father Nicholas Alexandrov of Moscow was arrested at the same time as the Dominican Sisters and sent to the Island of Solovki in the White Sea. Thirty-seven Russian Catholics were thus sent to prison; most of them were tried on May 24,

1924. Forty-three Orthodox, including several priests, were arrested at the same time for having established friendly relations with them.

Father Edmund Walsh left Russia at the end of November 1923, and a few weeks later the Pontifical Mission of Relief definitely closed its doors, the government considering that there was no longer any reason for its existence. Russia isolated herself more and more from the world.

The Catholics of Moscow soon found themselves without a pastor and the Catholics of Russia without a single bishop at liberty. The Holy See sent them, in secret, Bishop d'Herbigny to consecrate three bishops and later sent one of them, Bishop Pius Neveu, a French Assumptionist, to reside in Moscow. Prior to this, Mgr. Neveu had exercised his ministry in southern Russia. To prevent the Catholics from being accused of receiving their directives from prelates abroad, the Holy See gave full jurisdiction to Bishop Neveu over all Catholics living in Russia regardless of their rite. Thus Father Feodorov found himself henceforth placed under his immediate jurisdiction, yet the two prelates never had the opportunity to meet. From Moscow, Bishop Neveu tried to extend all possible fraternal aid to the Exarch, but at certain periods communication with the prisoners became almost impossible.

CHAPTER SIXTEEN

Kaluga: Three Months' Respite

In the meantime efforts were being made to obtain the release
of the Catholic prisoners. The Polish government in particular was interested in their fate, and at last reached an agreement whereby the Catholic priests of Polish origin were to be
exchanged for an equal number of Communist agents who
had been detained in Poland. So Archbishop Tseplyak and all
the priests of Latin rite were freed and returned to Poland,
while only Exarch Leonid remained in prison. Finally, Mrs.
Catherine Pyeshkov, wife of the writer Maxim Gorky, intervened on his behalf, as due to the popularity of her husband's
works at that time she had access to the Soviet leaders. She
pleaded with the GPU, emphasizing the injustice of keeping
Leonid Feodorov in prison while his thirteen companions,
sentenced for similar crimes, had been set free. "In fact," she
said, "he is being punished because he is Russian; if he were
Polish he would have been freed." She gave her personal
guarantee that the Exarch would observe any conditions imposed on him in exchange for his freedom, and eventually the
GPU gave in.

Father Leonid left prison in mid-April 1926, at the beginning of Holy Week, having spent three years in confinement. Even now he was not given complete liberty: the GPU put him in the class of citizens called 'except six,' which meant that he was forbidden to live in any of the six major cities of the country—Moscow, Leningrad, Odessa, Kharkov, Kiev or Rostov—or in any of the seaports, and that he also had to register every month with the police.

When he left prison he immediately made contact with the Russian Catholic parish in Moscow, the number of whose members had considerably diminished. The last Catholic Russian priest still at liberty, Father Serge Soloviov, had been deprived of the use of his chapel and had to celebrate the liturgy in a church of Latin rite. The Exarch joined him in saying the offices of Holy Week and Easter, and he was particularly touched by the warmth of the reception which he was given by the Catholic priests of Latin rite in Moscow.

On Easter Monday, May 2, he left for Kaluga, a city of roughly 100,000 inhabitants which lies about 100 miles southwest of Moscow. There he knew he had a friend whom he could trust. Three years before, the Catholic priest of Latin rite in Kaluga, a man of Lithuanian origin, Father John Pavlovich, had come specially to Moscow to attend the trial of Archbishop Tseplyak and his companions, and while listening to the proceedings he had been particularly impressed by the personality of the Exarch. Several times since he had gone to visit him in prison, and a friendship had sprung up between them based on their shared outlook and apostolic aspirations.

Actually Father Pavlovich could only stay in Kaluga for one week in each month; the other three he was obliged to spend visiting nine parishes which he had taken over when their priests were deported; and for this reason Father Leonid's help was most welcome. All the Catholics of Kaluga were

of Latin rite, and in the beginning they were disturbed by
their new priest who celebrated the offices in the same way as
those of the Orthodox Church; however, Father Pavlovich
reassured them when he returned from his pastoral journey.
In a letter written at this time, Father Leonid states: "Once
again I must repeat that the success of our work depends to a
great extent on the attitude towards us of our colleagues of
Latin rite . . ." [1] He himself knew the importance of not
keeping too rigid or formalistic an attitude: for example,
during the month of May he put on a Latin surplice and stole
to celebrate the votive offices in honor of the Virgin Mary in
the manner to which his parishioners of Latin rite were
accustomed.

The Exarch lost no time in continuing his work for the
Reunion of the Churches. He went to visit the bishop of the
Old Believers who was living in Kaluga, and also the city's
Orthodox priests. He arranged for the books he had left behind in Leningrad [formerly Petrograd] to be sent to him,
and he began to write apologetic pamphlets for use in his
apostolate. Finally, with the help of the Orthodox priests, in
particular Father Anthony Kobelev and a young philosopher
called Arkhangelsky, he organized lectures in defense of the
Christian faith against the militant atheists who were becoming increasingly powerful.

Unfortunately these activities were to last for a bare three
months. As soon as Father Bielogolov in Mohiliov learned
that the Exarch had been released from prison, he told him
that there was increasing interest in Reunion in the city, and
he asked him repeatedly to send a priest of Byzantine rite to
him for June 13, the feast of his church's patron, St. Anthony
of Padua. The Exarch had no priest whom he could send, so
he asked the local police for permission to go in person to
Mohiliov; the permission was granted, and he left at the
end of July. On his arrival he celebrated a solemn liturgy

and preached to the large crowd which had come to hear him.

The reaction of the GPU was immediate: a few hours later the Exarch and Father Bielogolov were arrested and thrown into prison. According to Father Pavlovich, in a letter written shortly after these arrests, they were based on a denunciation by the bishop of the so-called "Church of the Renovation," a break-away sect of the Orthodox Church.

Father Bielogolov was eventually executed, according to the GPU "while attempting to escape." Father Pavlovich was also arrested some time later and deported first to the far north and then to the Zyrian region of the Urals; here he disappeared and nothing is known of what became of him. As for the Exarch, after a short stay in the Liubianka prison in Moscow, he was condemned to three years deportation in the Solovki islands of the White Sea. He had been put in irons because he had left his place of residence without permission; when he pointed out that he had been given permission to go to Mohiliov by the Kaluga police, he was told that this was not sufficient, and that he should have asked for permission from the police in Moscow.

From this time on, the Exarch goes into a silence that is impressive for anyone who has examined the documents which he left. He had written a considerable amount; the large number of letters addressed to his friends, from the time of his stay in Anagni until the end of the three months he spent in Kaluga, make it easy for us to follow thus far the course of his life. Then suddenly all stops, and we have nothing more from him except a photograph with a few words written on it. This silence in itself gives some idea of the conditions under which he lived. All our information about him from that time onward comes from people who met him during his years as a convict.

What was his second trial like, and how was it conducted? Was he—like so many other people in Communist countries

—submitted to interrogations in which the judges take turns in examining the prisoner for several consecutive days and nights without giving him any rest or food? It is quite possible, but we do not know; he was unable to tell us.

CHAPTER SEVENTEEN

Deportation to the North

ALL things considered, the Exarch's first detention had not been very hard to bear; he had been classed with the Polish prisoners, and the GPU doubtless considered that it was better not to give the foreign press further opportunity to turn world opinion against it. But three years had now passed since the Moscow trial, the Soviets had strengthened their hold on the institutions of the country, the armies of their opponents had been defeated, and the Western Powers seemed to be resigned to the new regime established in Russia. As the Exarch was to learn to his cost, the Soviets were now able to use any methods they wished to subdue those who seemed not to accept their ideology with utter docility.

The prisoners condemned to be sent to the camps of the far north were piled into cattle cars, ironically nicknamed *tiepliuchki* (from the word *tieplo*, 'hot'; the nearest English translation would perhaps be 'chafing-dish'). Special trains made up of these cars left on fixed days in every week to take the convicts to their camps. In the main stations of Moscow and Leningrad special platforms had been prepared for them;

they were surrounded by barbed wire fences and watchtowers were placed at the four corners; they were guarded by soldiers armed with submachine guns, who would have shot down without pity anyone who made the slightest movement to escape.

In his memoirs, Mr. Boris Solonevitch, a former resident in one of these camps, writes: [1] "One might imagine that the maneuvers for embarking the prisoners in the trains, because of their frequency in Soviet Russia at the time, would have been carried out in a simple and orderly fashion. Instead of this, they were accompanied by cries, arguments and pushing, and all in indescribable confusion. The guards pushed the prisoners from one car to another until they found somewhere to get in. The escorts shouted, the common criminals fought among themselves, and the muzhiks, who had been deported for not showing enough enthusiasm when their farms were collectivized, moaned and wept. In general the *tiepliuchki* had been prepared for a cargo of forty men, but they usually carried sixty or seventy packed into them. None of these unfortunate people knew either where they were going or how long they would be shut up in their cages. . . . Along the walls of the cars there were wooden bunks, but there were not enough for everyone; they went to the strongest and were the subject of merciless battles. In this world the only law was that of the jungle, in other words, the most cynical egoism. Those who proved to be weak had to lie on the floor of the car, the boards of which were badly fitted and let through the icy wind of the north. Under the roof were four vents far above eye-level and blocked with thick iron bars. In the corner of the car a bucket served as a toilet and let off a repulsive odor at all times of the day and night."

The chief among the deportees were the kulaks, rich landowners who had fought against collectivization; there were a few intellectuals and workers, and finally the *urki,* the common criminals. At this time the *urki* were simply the dregs of the army of orphans and vagabonds who were everywhere in Russia. They always stayed together to attack and rob, and they had extraordinary powers of resistance.

"All those who have shown themselves unable to travel on train bumpers, to sleep on heaps of coal and to live off remains gathered from trash heaps—all these have died," continues Mr. Solonevich. "Only the toughest remain and they have unbelievable powers of survival; they are men who are filled with hatred for a world that threw them out in infancy on the highways of starvation and of the struggle for existence."

In such a world there was no possible recourse against violence. What did the soldiers in charge of the conveys care what happened in the cages? As long as none of the prisoners escaped and as long as the number of deaths during the journey was not more than average, they could live and enjoy themselves in peace. The food given to the convicts was just sufficient for them all not to die of starvation. Some among them went two or three days, and sometimes longer, without being given any food.

The Exarch was forced to suffer these conditions with the rest of the prisoners, but he was not able to describe them to us, and we do not know even how long the journey lasted. We do know, however, that these trains, driven by wood-fired locomotives, usually covered not more than 40 miles a day; so we have reason to fear that the Exarch spent about three weeks in these conditions, and possibly more. At the end of the journey the trains stopped at Kern, a little port on the White Sea. The prisoners were then transferred to a ship which took them finally to one of the islands of the Solovki archipelago. So Father Feodorov arrived on the principal island in mid-October 1926.

The archipelago of Solovki is situated on the same latitude

as Archangel and Iceland, and comprises a main island and six smaller ones, only one of which, Anser, is inhabited. At its widest point the main island measures 18 miles across. The islands are lined with hills and ravines, and covered with forests of pine and birch trees. They lie in the midst of the seas of the far north and consequently the climate is particularly unpleasant because it is both very cold and very humid. The sun rises for only a few minutes in the month of December, and during this time the islands are plunged in semi-darkness. On the other hand, in May and June there is no real night because the sun disappears only for a few minutes beneath the horizon. The average temperature over the whole year is not above 35° Fahrenheit; during the winter months the sea freezes and forms a thick ring of ice around each island which completely cuts it off.

No human being lived on the archipelago before 1439; in that year two monks of the Orthodox Church, St. Gherman and St. Savvati, went to the main island in search of solitude, and spent six years in isolation. In 1455 Savvati went back to the mainland where he died. His place was taken by a monk called Zosimus; others followed and began to build a wooden church and monastery. In 1588 the Higumen Philip, later to become Metropolitan of Moscow and to die by strangulation for opposing Ivan the Terrible, began to erect a huge stone monastery to which his remains were later brought from Moscow.

As the monastery was completely isolated, it had to defend itself against invaders, and successfully resisted attacks by the Swedish and the English. It gradually became a veritable military fortress as well as a center of prayer and culture in that harsh region of the north.

This oasis of spiritual and intellectual life the Soviets made into a concentration camp. The crosses which had formerly stood over the churches and the fortifications were torn down and replaced by the red flag. The monks were driven from their cells, their farms and their workshops; some of them were put in prison and those who remained, about sixty, were relegated to a few distant rooms of the monastery. At the same time the Soviets peopled these islands with thousands of prisoners, men, women and children who had been brought there in slow convoys from every part of the Soviet Union.

Along the walls and in the center of the former churches and halls, *nari* (camp beds) had been made by piling planks on top of each other. Early every morning guards came and, with rifle butts and shouts, awakened the prisoners sleeping on these plank beds. Shortly afterward the inmates left in caravans, regardless of cold weather or tempests or snow, to cut down trees in the forest, split them into logs, and transport them on their backs. Among these convicts were about a thousand "ministers of religion," Orthodox and Catholic bishops and priests, a few Protestant clergymen and Muslim muftis.

The Exarch was not the first Catholic priest to go to Solovki. In June 1924, while he was completing his first year's imprisonment, his priest in Moscow, Father Nicholas Alexandrov, together with two Dominican nuns and two Catholic laymen, had been arrested and deported by stages to the central island of the archipelago. The men were shut up with a hundred Orthodox priests in the central building called the Kremlin, and the women in a neighboring barrack.

The Orthodox priests on the island had obtained permission from the camp authorities to attend the liturgical services which the few remaining monks of Solovki who still had some degree of freedom celebrated in the chapel of the cemetery which had been left open for their use. Father Alexandrov asked for similar permission to be granted to the Catholics, and theoretically this was given, but with no practical result, for when the Catholics approached the monks with the request that they be allowed to use their chapel this was politely refused, and there was no place the Catholics could assemble.

In November 1925 the little group of Catholics of Byzantine rite gained three new members. They decided to appeal once more, and after praying fervently together they went to the head of the camp authorities with a concrete and definite request: they asked to be allowed to use an ancient chapel dedicated to St. Gherman, one of the original settlers of the island. This chapel was situated in an isolated spot on the seashore, at thirty minutes' walk from the Kremlin—a long way, but there was no other solution. The head of the camp had the reputation of being a cruel and sadistic man: it was rumored among the prisoners that he took actual pleasure in carrying out executions himself. However, he gave the necessary permission, although for only Sunday and feastdays, and on condition that each time the chapel was used a list of those who participated in or were present at the services should be given to the camp authorities.

The first office was celebrated in the chapel on Christmas 1925, and was followed by others on each Sunday and feastday. The Catholics met at a prearranged place in front of the Kremlin and went to the chapel together; on the way Father Nicholas heard confessions.

At first Father Nicholas had not wanted to celebrate the Eucharist without an antimension. At this time it was still possible for the prisoners to communicate with friends outside, and to receive parcels containing food and clothing. Hearing of Father Nicholas' dilemma, a Catholic woman in Moscow managed to tell Rome of the situation and to convey to him the reply of the Holy See: the Pope gave permission to priests who were in prison and unable to obtain an antimension to celebrate the Eucharist on an ordinary piece of cloth, provided they conveyed themselves in spirit to the tombs of the nearest saints. The same woman managed to send Father Nicholas a parcel containing eucharistic wine, and shortly afterward she sent an antimension and then icons and silk for liturgical vestments. When the Catholics first got permission to use it, St. Gherman's chapel had only its four walls. Two years later, thanks to the ingenuity and patience of the faithful, it was transformed; it had an altar, icons, books, and four liturgical vestments with the necessary accessories.

Before his ordination Father Nicholas had been a skilled electrical engineer. His jailers in Solovki learned of his abilities and called increasingly on his services for the needs of this vast camp. The priest took advantage of this to ask in return for new concessions for the use of the chapel. Eventually he got permission to hold services not only on Sundays and feastdays but also during the week, and began to celebrate the Divine Liturgy every morning. To do this he had to get up at 5 o'clock and walk for half an hour in each direction in the darkness, the cold and the snow. Sister Imelda, one of the Dominican nuns from Moscow, went with him to give the responses, and generally a few of the faithful joined them. They acknowledged later that in the winter their pilgrimage to the chapel had been prevented only three times by bad weather.

The first priest of Latin rite, Father Baranovsky, dean of Vitebsk, arrived on Solovki during the summer of 1926. From then on liturgical services were arranged also for the Catholics of Latin rite. There was a certain amount of trouble with the minor officials of the camp, but the engineer-priest, Father Nicholas, always managed to straighten things out. Theoretically St. Gherman's chapel was only to be used by the *tzerkovniki,* those who had been sentenced for their religious activities, but in practice many other prisoners managed to attend services there.

The Exarch's sudden arrival on the island during the month of October was an event of major importance for the little Catholic group. He was unable to join them at once because the authorities kept him in quarantine for two weeks. One of his companions of the time tells us: "In spite of this we managed to give him what was necessary to celebrate the Eucharist, and when he came out of quarantine, he joined us at St. Gherman. When he preached it was with such depth of understanding and with so much conviction that the courage of the prisoners was greatly strengthened . . ."

Propaganda for atheism and pressure against all religious organizations was growing daily in Russia, with the result that during the summer of 1927 there was a considerable increase in the number of Catholic prisoners. Among the new arrivals were two Catholic priests of Byzantine rite, one of them a Georgian archimandrite, and about twenty priests of Latin rite. Such a large group could no longer go every morning to St. Gherman, so the Catholics tried to arrange to be housed together in the same cells, so that they could celebrate liturgical services and pray together, using suitcases piled one on top of the other as an altar. On Sundays those who could went to St. Gherman; a choir was organized and they arranged to celebrate the Eucharistic sacrifice alternately in the Latin and in the Byzantine rite.

Thanks to the generosity of distant friends they were able to add constantly to the ornaments of the chapel. One day a portable Latin altar, with four full sets of vestments, arrived in a parcel. Food parcels sent by friends who were still free usually contained a small quantity of liturgical wine. Moreover, the Orthodox monks of the Solovki monastery began to help the Catholics, their early reserve and suspicion having gradually given place to a friendly attitude. Among other things, they procured a mitre for the Exarch so that he could celebrate services with the proper marks of his rank.

The slightly different attitudes of the Catholic and the Orthodox priests imprisoned at Solovki were a consequence of the differing tendencies of Western and Eastern spirituality. The Catholic priests had been trained to a more individualist attitude in spiritual matters, and for them the Eucharistic sacrifice was a personal support; they found themselves united with Christ who made them present sacramentally at His passion; the number of people present and the surroundings were of little importance to them. Later they were often to have only a tiny, rough stole in which to celebrate Mass, using a simple glass and a disk of iron as a chalice and paten. The Orthodox Christians, on the other hand, continued to consider the Divine Liturgy more as a collective action of the Christian family; in general they did not presume to celebrate it through pure personal devotion without the usual vestments and solemnity, and without being in some way the delegates of a community.

In 1927 a rumor reached the Catholics who were confined to Solovki: one of the three bishops whom Bishop d'Herbigny had consecrated in private, Mgr. Boleslav Sloskan, had been arrested by the GPU. Without being a prophet, anyone could foresee that he too would one day be sent to Solovki. However, it was not until a year later that this prediction became a reality. Meanwhile, the bishop was given hard work to do in the region of Uchta, on the continental coast not far from Solovki. Exhausted, crippled by rheumatism, now deaf, he was finally sent to Solovki with a party of sick men. He arrived on August 12, 1928, and was abandoned without medical care in a corridor of the hospital. On the third day, an Orthodox monk who had become a nurse discovered him.

"You are a bishop!" he exclaimed. "I didn't know that!" He at once found a place for Bishop Sloskan in a room and did all he could to see that he had the necessary food and medicine. The bishop regained his strength and with it his hearing, and the pain in his leg disappeared. The Catholics were informed, and a few days later, the Exarch, accompanied by a layman from Moscow, D.N., approached the bishop when no one was looking. The Exarch told him about the liturgical life organized on the island and of the fervor of the Catholics, and he immediately asked him if he would ordain to the priesthood a candidate whom he had carefully prepared. Everything had been foreseen. Convinced that one day or other Bishop Sloskan would rejoin them, the Catholics had secured the Pontifical * from Moscow and all that was necessary for ordinations to the priesthood. On September 5 a small group of faithful who had been secretly informed went to the chapel of St. Gherman, and at four in the morning D.N. was ordained deacon. Two days later he was ordained priest under the same conditions.

After three years of deportation in Siberia, Miss Danzas was also sent to Solovki. Her journey with groups of prisoners from Irkutsk to the islands of the White Sea lasted four months and she arrived on August 29, 1928. To her immense joy, she learned from the Dominican Sisters from Moscow who were prisoners on the island that the Exarch was also there. However, because of the separation made between the groups of prisoners, she was able only once to go to the chapel of St. Gherman. This was on a Sunday and Father Feodorov was celebrating the Sacred Liturgy. His former secretary was amazed to see how ill he looked; he was again suffering from rheumatism and tortured by swollen legs. She was able to speak to him afterward only briefly, for he had to return to the huts before the morning call.

However, she later managed to see him for a longer period of time. Shortly after her arrival, Miss Danzas was attached as an accountant to a museum where curious objects collected

* Liturgical book for ritual of ordinations to the priesthood in the Latin rite.

in the ancient monastery were on exhibition. As a matter of fact, very few of them remained, the most precious having been stolen during the general pillage which had occurred during the early years of the Revolution. The prisoners were allowed to visit the museum; they were led in groups of fifty, and a guide gave an antireligious talk on the objects. One day the Exarch managed to join one of these groups and at the right moment left it to speak freely with the museum's accountant, Miss Danzas, who was supposed to give him a detailed course in antireligion! The accomplice had been a young jailer familiar to the prisoners as Dimka, the diminutive of Dimitri. This twenty-year-old boy was actually a sworn enemy of Communism, and when his true feelings were revealed a year later he was shot.

According to Miss Danzas, on the occasion of their meeting the Exarch seemed profoundly affected by the collapse of all his work. He considered himself responsible and attributed this to his unworthiness and incapacity. Their meeting lasted three hours. With profound respect, the Exarch kissed a vestment which had once been worn by the holy Metropolitan Philip, the victim of Ivan the Terrible, and the stone on which the saint had rested his head. "On this stone," the Exarch recalled, "the saint had not only radiant visions, but how many bitter tears did he shed!" Then turning to Miss Danzas, he continued, "No doubt you too have undergone some painful periods."

"Yes," she replied. "You know that. But since my long stay at the Irkutsk prison, I have regained peace and clarity."

"That is well," said the Exarch. "The Lord will sustain you, but if ever the moment returns when you no longer feel this support, don't be frightened. The Lord's aid is perhaps precisely the most abundant when it seems that he has forsaken us." [2]

The Father had to leave in haste; Dimka came to speak to

him as he wanted him to be present at the evening call in his hut.

During these three hours with Miss Danzas, the Exarch had not spoken of any question of a temporary order; he had seemed lost in God. "The true messianism of the Russian Church," he emphasized, "is not what the Slavophiles have imagined, but it is the example of suffering. It is in this way that she shows that she is the continuation of Christ in this world."

CHAPTER EIGHTEEN

Solovki and the Isle of Anser

THE winter nights never seemed to end in the Great North. When darkness fell upon the forests, cutting down trees was no longer possible and the prisoners killed time together in their huts. The Catholic priests often found themselves mingling with the elite members of the Orthodox clergy, that is, with the priests and bishops who, in spite of the dangers, were not afraid to confess their faith. The Exarch, more than anyone else, acted as liaison between the two groups; in fact, he was truly at home in both. Consequently, thanks to him, ecumenical and theological conferences took place on certain evenings in that austere northern solitude. Their value and cordiality exceeded anything that could have been organized elsewhere at that time in the Christian world.

Should this surprise us? Conversation often reached the crucial question between Orthodox and Catholic, namely, the pastoral primacy of the Bishop of Rome and his infallibility on doctrinal matters. Among the Orthodox prisoners was Archbishop Ilarion Troitzky, Patriarch Tikhon's former auxiliary bishop and righthand man, the same who in 1922 had presided in Moscow at the two conferences between Catholics and Orthodox organized by the Orthodox themselves. According to Bishop Sloskan, who was present at the meeting, Archbishop Ilarion was an obstinate adversary of papal infallibility. The dialogue between him and the Exarch was therefore very close-set. However, it was evident that the Orthodox bishop had formed an inaccurate interpretation of authentic Catholic teaching on this very point. The Exarch tried to make him understand, but how could he prove that his assertions expressed the true doctrine of the Roman Church?

It was then that the old monks of Solovki came to his aid. Among the many books in the monastery library which they had managed to hide, they discovered a few works which the Exarch had been seeking. The exact point of their disagreement has not been reported, but we know that after reading the text which the Exarch produced and listening to his explanation, Archbishop Ilarion laid down his arms that night. "Understood in this manner," he stated, "I can no longer see why this dogma could not be accepted by the Eastern world." [1]

The eucharistic and liturgical life maintained a moral vigor among the Catholic prisoners of the two rites which surprised their companions. The conditions to which they were subjected had been organized to discourage them: the food was plain and monotonous, the work in the forests and in the snow was exhausting. They were separated from those they loved in this world; mail was increasingly difficult to receive, and moreover the news itself from the outside world was extremely depressing: antireligious propaganda was growing throughout Russia. "By casting us on these inhospitable islands," one of them reported, "the GPU had hoped that we would soon succumb to a common fate, that is, that we would break down, become depressed and terrorized like the other prisoners. But this did not happen, thanks to the liturgical life which we managed to organize and for which we then enjoyed, providentially, enough freedom. The GPU was convinced that our spirit of joy, peace and resignation, which they called our 'pride,' would soon vanish. Time taught them the contrary. Accustomed to dealing with prisoners oppressed by fear, the agents of the GPU were obviously irritated by our spirit of independence. One day one of them exclaimed, "To see the way they are acting, you would think we were dealing with the British Ambassador!" "Others," the same witness wrote, "thought that they had explained everything by pretending that a Jesuit was hidden among the prisoners!" [2]

By showing themselves provisionally rather tolerant, the agents of the GPU had a secret purpose: they hoped that the leaders of the group would become more and more daring and reveal themselves; thus they could get rid of them. The priests were the objects of constant spying, but the results were often the very opposite of what the jailers expected. For example, one day an Orthodox priest was given the order to spy on some Catholic priests. After that he sought to be on intimate terms with them, but eventually he abandoned the despicable task which he had assumed and even expressed the desire to be received into the Catholic Church.

About November 1, 1928, there came a dramatic turn of events: the Orthodox and Catholic chapels were closed. Urgent appeals were made but the director of the prison camps refused to alter his decision. The Catholic priests therefore organized to celebrate the Eucharistic sacrifice secretly in their huts, but this meant that the faithful were deprived of the Eucharist. The prisoners returned to the customs of the catacombs and of the primitive Church. Sister Imelda, one of the Dominican Sisters of Moscow, was a nurse at the hospital and therefore enjoyed a certain liberty to mingle among the prisoners in order to visit the sick. She

used to go and see the priests who would hand her consecrated Hosts which had been carefully wrapped in small
sheets of paper. The Sisters would meet in one of their huts,
read together the daily office, and would consume the holy
species without touching them.

On January 19, 1929, during a frightfully cold night, a
large group of police suddenly appeared on the premises occupied by the Orthodox and Catholic clergy. Everything that
could be used for religious services was pitilessly confiscated:
vestments, sacred vessels, books, flour, wine, even the smallest
icons. The priests were made to take their bundles of clothing
and leave their common hut to be scattered among the other
prisoners. Thus it would be almost impossible for them to
celebrate their religious offices.

The search and the change of hut took more than four
hours. At two o'clock in the morning, the police finally left.
There now remained only four men: Bishop Sloskan, two
priests and a trustworthy layman. They glanced at each other
and began to take stock of what they had lost and what had
escaped the myrmidons. As luck would have it, there remained the bare necessities for celebrating the Eucharistic
sacrifice. Bishop Sloskan did not hesitate. "Brothers," he
stated solemnly, "let us at once celebrate holy Mass!" "We
did so without hesitation," reported one of the priests who
was present. "I think that of all the bold acts we ever committed at Solovki, this crowned them all." And he added,
"These were the good old days and I am pleased to have spent
them at Solovki."

"From that time on," the same witness continued, "we
really descended into the catacombs. . . . I asked the Exarch
if we had to celebrate the Holy Sacrifice under the threat of
painful sanctions. He replied in these memorable words, 'Do
not forget that the Divine Liturgies we are celebrating at
Solovki are perhaps the only ones which the Catholic priests

of the Russian rite are still celebrating on Russian soil for
Russia. Everything must be done so that at least one Liturgy
is celebrated daily.' "

To those around him and who suffered with him, Father
Leonid continued to express the profound conviction which
had sustained him since his years at Anagni: "All the powers
of hell have been loosed to prevent the reconciliation of dis-
united Christians. The apostle of Reunion can vanquish them
only by sacrificing himself completely with the Redeemer.
By natural forces alone, Church unity cannot be achieved."

Each priest then tried to adapt himself to the particular
situation in which he found himself. Father Nicholas Alexandrov celebrated the Divine Liturgy in a solitary corner of
the electrical center, another priest celebrated it in the
carpentry shop. However, many priests were occupied in
rougher tasks, especially that of dragging carts of wood over
long distances. As it was a Soviet practice to form new words
by juxtaposing the first letters, the priests, not without a
certain humor, used to call this kind of work *"vridlo,"* from
the first letters of the Russian words, *"Vremennoie ispolnenie
doljnostei lochadi,"* which means "temporary fulfilment of a
horse's functions."

At Easter of 1929 the Russian Catholics achieved a small
victory. The Orthodox and the Jews had received permission
to celebrate their feastdays openly. The Catholic group proceeded to make what one of the members called "some energetic requests" in order to obtain the same right. This was
finally granted and they were allowed to celebrate the services
in a small chapel dedicated to Philip, the holy Metropolitan of Moscow. The Catholics of the Latin rite were the
only ones who could not celebrate; that year the permission
came too late, due to the difference of the calendars; the
Easter of the Latin Catholics was already over. Therefore they
joined their brothers of the Eastern rite and this Easter lit-

urgy concelebrated by the Exarch and his priests was the last Catholic liturgy to be celebrated in public at Solovki.

During the search on the night of January 19, Exarch Feodorov had been assigned to the 13th company of prisoners, one which in the slang of the island was known as the "Cesspool of Solovki." The buildings which had been assigned to this company were supposed to hold a group of 100 to 150 prisoners, whereas that winter more than 2,000 were sent there. The other buildings were also overcrowded; at that time, there were 26,000 prisoners thrown practically one on top of the other in premises which should not have held more than 5,000 to 6,000. One-third of these unfortunate prisoners died of typhus during the winter which followed.

After Easter of that year, the Exarch's state of health became considerably worse. He was finally admitted to the hospital, and thus found himself temporarily separated from the other priests.

On June 9 of that year they suffered another cruel blow. An administrative decision forced all the ecclesiastics to leave for the second island of the archipelago, the Island of Anser. On disembarking at the island, their bundles of clothing were very carefully examined, but strangely enough neither the books nor the liturgical vestments attracted the guards' attention. The relocation of the prisoners, carried out by orders and counterorders, took ten days. Finally, the bishop and the priests were sent to the same place, a small loft. To their unexpected joy, they found themselves together again. With them was an Orthodox bishop and a priest of the Orthodox Ukrainian Church separated from the Russian Church. In all they were twenty at the beginning, but shortly afterward they were joined by three new prisoners. One of them has recorded for posterity the exact dimensions of the small loft: it was 12 feet in length, 8 feet in width, and 8 feet 9 inches in height; thus there were three prisoners per square yard!

And yet even in such unfavorable conditions the priests returned to celebrating the holy Eucharistic sacrifice. "We celebrated first under an open sky," one of them wrote, "in the forest which suited us quite well. In fact, we had discovered a large flat stone which we used as an altar. Bishop Sloskan was the first to celebrate there. However, as storms were frequent in that region, celebration became impossible. It was then decided that the holy Eucharistic sacrifice would be celebrated on the ledges of the dormer windows of the roof. However, they were so low that the priest had to kneel during the entire celebration."

The major obstacle to the celebration at this time became the lack of liturgical wine. Although a few parcels still arrived from the outside world, the wine which they contained was generally confiscated. The priests tried secretly to acquire some by giving a remuneration either to the administrative agents or to the sailors, but the bottles were often half emptied en route.

Then one of the priests remembered that according to the theological manuals of Tanquerey it was permissible to make altar wine with raisins. The priests sent for some; dipped into lukewarm water, the raisins again acquired their original size. Pressed, they gave a juice which after fermentation became genuine wine. One of the priests among the prisoners became a real specialist in the preparation of this wine. United in a kind of small local council, Bishop Sloskan and the priests decided that in order to celebrate the Eucharistic sacrifice, they would use only six to eight drops of wine to which, according to custom, they would add a drop of water.

In July Father Leonid, who was in the hospital, had recovered enough to return to the camp. He then rejoined his brother priests on the Isle of Anser and was sent to work with them in the forests. During the entire day he again had to cut down trees, to prune and saw them. He also had to pick up from the sea wood which had been cast ashore by storms. More painful still was the work of digging the foundation for the erection of new prisons or the preparation of common burial ditches, for the clay soil mingled with huge stones was frozen during almost the entire year.

After a few weeks, the Exarch's three-year prison term expired. At the end of 1929, he bade farewell to his companions and gained the continent. Meanwhile, Miss Danzas had been removed from her museum and deported also to the Isle of Anser for clandestine religious propaganda. "From the women's hut where I was confined," she wrote, "I saw the Exarch pass by with all his belongings. Alas, it was impossible to meet even for a glance." [3]

CHAPTER NINETEEN

The Last Years

By the terms of the Exarch's sentence, his three years of imprisonment at Solovki were to be followed by three years of deportation in the north. He was therefore transferred to a small village made up of a cluster of isbas (log huts) near Pinega, a town of only 2,000 inhabitants isolated in the tundra about 200 miles east of Archangel.

He gained nothing by the transfer from the point of view of climate, for Pinega is on almost the same latitude as the archipelago of Solovki. But agriculture and cattle-raising are somewhat more developed there, and in addition to them fishing and fur trading provide the inhabitants with a reasonable income.

Father Leonid arranged simply for a room to be reserved for him in a farmer's isba, and he had as a fellow-lodger Father Parphene Kruglikov, an Orthodox priest who had been punished with the same sentence. To earn his living, the Exarch helped the farmers and hunters of the district.

A small sum of money was sent to him by the Catholics in Leningrad and Moscow, but parcels were rare. Many of his friends had been arrested, and those who were still free were afraid to compromise themselves, especially if they had families dependent on them. It was becoming increasingly dangerous even to send letters to "ministers of religion" who had been deported or were suspect. By this time Stalin had eliminated Trotsky and his other rivals and had become the pitiless dictator of the Soviet Union, feared by even his closest colleagues. Religious persecution was worse than ever before. Those priests who had not been arrested had their nerves shattered; the police kept them in a state of constant tension by searching their homes at any hour of the day or night, and submitting them to long periods of capricious and arbitrary cross-questioning.

This was the time that Pope Pius XI with other Church leaders intervened forcefully on behalf of Russian believers. On February 2, 1930, the Pope wrote a public letter to Cardinal Pompili, who was in charge of St. Peter's Basilica in Rome, inviting him to organize a ceremony of expiation at St. Peter's "for the horrible and sacrilegious crimes, which are repeated and grow worse each day, against God and against the souls of the many different peoples of Russia, all of whom are dear to our heart were it only because of the greatness of their suffering . . ."

Pius XI went on to recall how at the Conference of Genoa he had asked the governments represented there to make a unanimous declaration which would have spared much misery in Russia and in the rest of the world; namely, to proclaim respect for consciences, freedom of worship and respect for church property as necessary conditions for recognition of the Soviet government. He also mentioned that these three conditions, from which Orthodox believers would have gained more than anyone, were not made to the Soviet government through concern for material interests.

Later in the letter the Pope sent his greetings to all the

priests and members of religious orders who had been deported, and in particular to "our representative for the Slavonic rite, the Catholic Exarch Leonidas Feodorov."

In Pinega, Father Leonid was able to celebrate the Divine Liturgy in private. He had become a friend of the priest in charge of the local Orthodox church and was very happy to be able to borrow his small collection of books so that he could spend the long evenings of the eight months of winter profitably.

There was at that time at Pinega a Latin rite Catholic priest, Father Vincent Ilguin, who had also been deported for religious activity. Later Father Ilguin was freed and allowed to go to Poland. He was able, therefore, to write us a few details about the Exarch; they are doubly precious because the two priests had already spent two years together in the barracks of Solovki.

"When I met the Exarch for the first time," writes Father Vincent, "he made on me the most agreeable impression. He was a man of great intelligence; his face, with very regular features, was accented by a lightly tinted red beard; his eyes were very clear and full of life. His conversation flowed freely, was always rich in content and invariably aroused interest among the listeners. When we were free from our forced labor, we liked to gather around him; he attracted us by his kindness, his simplicity, his cordiality. He was distinguished by an exceptional courtesy and an unlimited, artless simplicity.

"When his turn came to be on guard at the door or when we met him with a broom in his hands cleaning around the barracks, he was always smiling and gracious. . . . When he saw that others were depressed, he urged them to be patient and he cheered them up by awakening in them hope for better times. If in exile he received some material help, he used to divide it with the others. . . . In the camps the food was unvaried and tasteless, but Father Leonid had found a way of offering friends who called on him something a little tastier than usual; he had become a specialist in preparing tea." "He used to say," writes Father Vincent further, "that his tea was much better than anywhere else because he alone was able to make what the Russians call 'tea with a cock' (*tshayok s pietushkom*), meaning by this that he could put on his teapot a cozy which kept the water warmer and secured therefore a stronger brewing of the tea." "He was right," writes Father Ilguin, "this tea was delicious and we drank it with great pleasure." This would have been insignificant in other circumstances, but in Pinega as in Solovki it showed a strong will to overcome the depressing influence of the gloomy surroundings and brought some warmth and a new courage to many.

"The Bolsheviks," continues Father Vincent, "tried many times to win the Exarch to their ideology. They tried to do this with all the prisoners but mostly with the priests. The clergy as a general rule showed themselves inflexible, but Father Leonid was more staunch than anybody else; the Bolshevik minions learned soon that they would always find in him an invincible soldier of Christ." [1]

After Father Leonid left Pinega the local Orthodox pastor used to say that if the Exarch had remained in his parish, he would have taken away most of his parishioners.

The Pinega section of the GPU kept watch on the Exarch's activities, and early in 1931 wanted to force him to drag trucks with wood in the forest and again to dig ditches. Father Leonid refused and pointed out that as a political prisoner he could not be obliged to do manual labor; moreover, his state of health no longer enabled him to undertake such work. The GPU persisted and finally Father Leonid was arrested and sent to prison in Archangel; he stayed there for six months until a favorable reply came from the higher authorities in Moscow in answer to the protest which he had sent them. He was released from prison, but he was still obliged to continue his three years' deportation in the north. So in the autumn of 1931 the Exarch was able to go to Kotlas, an important railroad center. At the headwaters of the Dvina, the main river of northern Russia which flows into the White Sea, this city stays open to shipping throughout the year, so the climate is slightly less harsh. Father Leonid lodged in the village of Poltava, 10 miles to the south of Kotlas, where a small corner was reserved for him in the isba of two old farmers. He had a bed, a table and a stool; there was a curtain which gave him a minimum of privacy and a certain amount of solitude. In Poltava, as in Solovki and Pinega, he loved to join his suffering to those of Christ through often celebrating the Eucharistic sacrifice. In the hospital of Kotlas he found a Catholic nurse, Mrs. Catherine N., whose special work was to care for sick prisoners in their huts. She was happy to meet a priest, and kept the Exarch regularly informed of the names of Catholic deportees. Under various pretexts, he went to see them and brought them the sacraments of the Church.

While in Kotlas, the Exarch had the great consolation of a visit from one of his priests, Father E.A., who had recently been released from prison and resided in Leningrad. The young priest came to spend a few days with Father Leonid at the request of Bishop Pius Neveu, the French Assumptionist who was then the only Catholic priest residing in Moscow.

In Kotlas the Exarch did not forget his Polish friend Father Vincent Ilguin who had been left alone in Pinega. He used to write him faithfully twice a month: "These letters," Father Ilguin wrote later, "were real spiritual food in my exile. They brought me an addition of courage and strength to bear the weight and trials of everyday life."

This stay in the region of Kotlas lasted two years. Father Leonid was stricken with new acute bouts of rheumatism and with very painful gastritis. When she learned of his state of health, Mrs. Catherine Pyeshkov, wife of the writer Maxim Gorky, agreed to intervene on his behalf as she had done in 1926 during his first imprisonment. The Exarch was granted his freedom, but he was put in the category known as 'except twelve,' which meant that he was not allowed to live in any of the twelve largest cities of the Soviet Union or in the regions near the frontier or the sea.

In the early days of January 1934, the Exarch left Kotlas and settled for the time being 250 miles to the south in the town of Viatka, which at the end of that year was to be re-named Kirov, after a protégé of Stalin's who was assassinated in Leningrad on December 1, 1934.

The Exarch lodged with a man named Andrew Kalinin who worked in the railway station. He payed 10 rubles a month to occupy a corner of the one room where this worker lived with his wife and three children. Later the Exarch intended to move to Smolensk or Yaroslav where the climate was milder.

Early in February, he developed a continual cough; he lost much strength and no longer ate the bread and tea which were his usual diet. He became too weak to get out of bed. A doctor named Molchanov came regularly to see him, and at each visit the Exarch thanked him warmly. Mr. Kalinin tells us, in some notes which he wrote regarding Father Leonid's last days, that he never complained.

On Wednesday March 6, at about 5.00 p.m., the doctor came to see him for the last time. No doubt to encourage him, he left his patient a prescription, but as he was going he told Mrs. Kalinin privately that her lodger had not long to live.

The next day, March 7, at 11.00 a.m., Father Leonid asked for a glass of warm milk. When he had drunk it, he said: "Now I shall sleep for at least two hours."

"My wife had to go into town," Mr. Kalinin writes, "and she asked the sick man if he needed anything, but he seemed to stare without answering. His hands lay on his chest, the right hand uppermost. My wife called me and said: "I think he is dying. . . ." We were standing round him. I called him and said, "Please tell me what we ought to do; do you feel ill? You don't say anything, as if you were going to die. . . ." But he remained with his eyes open, without moving his eyelids and without saying anything; the color drained from his face. Then we realized that he had stopped breathing. . . ."

"We waited until two o'clock in the afternoon without touching him. We did not know what to do because he had given us no instructions. We did not know whom to tell of his death. Finally we washed him, dressed him in clean linen and laid him out in our apartment. We did not want to give his body to the morgue near the town hospital. . . ."

"On March 10 (a Sunday), when we had carried out all the necessary formalities, we buried him at eight o'clock in the evening, in the dark, doing everything which should be done in such circumstances. . . ."

This last sentence, which seems deliberately vague, suggests that the Exarch's body was not buried without a prayer. Whether his grave was blessed by a priest that evening, we do not know.

CHAPTER TWENTY

Victory in Failure

As soon as they were informed on the Exarch's death, the police came to take possession of everything which he had written during his last months. From March 7 to 10 his body had lain in a corner of the isba, while outside the cold of the north could be felt in all its harshness. On one occasion the Kalinin children left the door of the house open, and it happened that a dove came into the room, flew around Father Leonid's body, and left as it had entered. Those who had come to pray near the dead man were surprised and moved by this incident, and the Kalinins, also impressed, made special mention of it in the report which they wrote on the Exarch's death.

In March 1935, Bishop Pius Neveu sent a Russian Catholic woman from Moscow to offer the Exarch any material help possible. When she arrived in Viatka, Father Leonid had left this world, but she was able to collect the above details about his last days.

All the Exarch's close collaborators suffered imprisonment in concentration camps, and they died one after the other.

After his arrest in 1923, Father Alexis Zerchaninov, despite his 75 years, was deported to Tobolsk. There he had the comfort of being able to baptize secretly some Siberian fishermen whom Mrs. Abrikosov's Dominican Sisters, who had also been deported to Siberia, had converted to Christ. He died in the house of one of his sons at Gorky (formerly Nizhni-Novgorod) on September 23, 1933, at the age of 85, while he was on the way back to Leningrad.

Father Deibner was condemned to 10 years of hard labor, and the circumstances of his death are not known precisely, though it appears that he was mortally wounded by one of his fellow-prisoners. Father Potapii died early in 1937 at Poidvoitzi, a stop on the Murmansk railroad. Father Sergius Soloviov died of exhaustion in Moscow; Father E.A., who had spent eight years as a deportee, was arrested again after a period of freedom; from then on we can find no further trace of him.

Mother Catherine of Siena, whose name in the world was Mrs. Abrikosov, was arrested with most of her Sisters in 1923. First she underwent in Moscow four months of solitary confinement, then she was put into a cell with a number of her religious; she was later deported with some of them to Tobolsk. After six years in exile she was brought back to Yaroslav in Europe. As she was found to have a cancerous tumor she was transferred in July 1932 to the infirmary of the Butyrka prison in Moscow, where Bishop Neveu made several unsuccessful attempts to see her. On August 12, 1932, she was set free, but in August 1933 she was once more arrested for teaching religion to young people, and again sent to the Yaroslav prison. There in 1935 the tumor began to affect her face; she was transferred to a Moscow prison where she died on June 23, 1936.

As we have already mentioned, the publicist Dimitri Kuzmine-Karavaiev had been expelled from Russia in 1922.

After a short stay in Berlin and Paris, he went to Rome, and there entered the Greek seminary. At the age of 35, he began to study and he was ordained priest on July 3, 1927. From then until his death in Rome on March 16, 1959, he filled various pastoral and teaching posts in Berlin, Louvain, Namur and Paris.

Miss Danzas was freed from Solovki in 1933, and a year later she left Russia. She lived in France writing books and articles which aroused considerable interest, and she died in Rome on April 13, 1942. Early in 1964, as these lines are written, only one of the Exarch's close associates is still alive: Father Vladimir Abrikosov, now in his eighties, who lives as a hermit in a room in the Auteuil dstrict of Paris, spending his time in prayer.

So far the Exarch for the Catholic Russians has had no successor; there seems to be nothing left of his exarchate . . . at first sight it might appear that his immense efforts ended in complete failure. Certainly had Father Feodorov's aim been to organize in Russia a new group in competition with the national Orthodox Church, one could hardly call the result a success. But his objective was much higher. In his letters to Pope Pius XI and before his judges in Moscow, he proclaimed with clearness and emphasis: "My chief idea has been to reconcile my country with the Catholic Church . . ."

To actualize this plan, it was indispensable that Christian Russia, with all her liturgical, ascetical and theological traditions, be known and rightly appreciated in the Catholic world. If, thirty years after his death, we look at his work from this point of view, would it be untrue to say that a real victory is emerging from his struggle? When, in the first days of the twentieth century, Leonid Feodorov went to Rome to study for the priesthood, there was in Russia a Catholic hierarchy and hundreds of Latin rite Catholic priests were scattered over the whole of the Empire. But at that time by far the greater majority—if not all—of these bishops and priests were convinced that Russia could become fully Catholic only by renouncing its ancestral traditions and adopting the Roman rite —and they would have found support in several influential circles in Rome.

Less than thirty years later, the situation had changed completely. There was no longer any doubt about the subject: the fact that there had existed in Russia a tiny community of truly Russian Catholics led by an outstanding pastor brought the Catholic Church to a fuller awareness of its universal mission and has helped it to overcome the temptation to limit itself to a sort of Latin parochialism. The facts are eloquent in themselves. In 1929 a Russian seminary was opened in Rome; in order to gain admission to it, the candidates must express the desire to be ordained in the Byzantine rite. In this seminary they are trained to follow this rite in its purest traditions. To help them, the Holy See has had the necessary liturgical books very carefully printed.

At Chèvetogne, in Belgium, in the Prieuré de l'Union (Priory for Unity), a group of Benedictine monks are trying through liturgical life in the Byzantine rite to explore the riches of the Eastern monastic traditions and to make them better known in the Catholic world mostly through their periodical and the books which they publish. This monastery is a living witness to the Catholic Church's concern for the Christian East and in particular for Russia, and also for corporate Reunion. Many Russians have fled from Russia to escape the Soviet regime. To help their children, the Marian Fathers opened a school in Harbin, Manchuria, while the Jesuits, the Ursulines and the Ladies of St. Clotilde have organized boarding schools in Shanghai, Paris, Meudon, São Paulo and Santos. In all these Russian Catholic schools, priests and teachers follow the Byzantine rite and teach the children to pray in Church Slavonic according to their ancestral traditions. They try to educate these Russian Orthodox children in loyal collaboration with the Orthodox clergy.

The progress that has been made in a few decades may be judged by some other facts. In 1922 when Benedict XV received from Patriarch Tikhon a handwritten appeal for help for those suffering from starvation, the Pope—to the great sorrow of the Russian Catholics *—decided to reply only through his Secretary of State. In 1963 the situation had changed completely. Pope John XXIII exchanged several personal letters and telegrams with the Patriarch of Moscow, and invited the Russian Orthodox Church to send observers to Vatican Council II, an invitation that was accepted. A Russian Orthodox delegation was present at the coronation of Pope John's successor, Pope Paul VI, and the new Pope sent the Swiss Bishop François Charrière and a well-known ecumenist, the Very Reverend Christophe Dumont, O.P. of Paris, to take his personal greeting to Patriarch Alexis on the occasion of the latter's episcopal jubilee. And did not the same Pope's moving meetings with Patriarch Athanagoras in the Holy Land, in January 1964, open up new vistas of understanding and sympathy with all the Eastern Churches? In short the Catholic world has rapidly come to share the open and generous beliefs of Exarch Feodorov.

Perhaps one might summarize, therefore, the first fruits of his efforts by saying that, thanks to him and to his little flock, Russia with her Christian traditions has finally received not only in theory but in fact her full right of citizenship in the Catholic Church. This is a first victory and a first step which was necessary for the reunion of the two Churches.

Will the Exarch also win the Orthodox world to his point of view? Even if at present he is unknown to it, perhaps

* See p. 131.

these pages describing his life will introduce him to his
compatriots and win for him the esteem that is due to one
of such outstanding moral stature.

This will not be easy. In general the Russians have some
aversion for those among them who go over to the Catholic
Church; they readily suspect them of being moved by worldly
motives. Who could be less open to such a suspicion than
Father Feodorov? At the age of twenty he left his widowed
mother alone and his beloved country to spend long years
studying in exile, leading a hard and ascetic life. No sooner
did he return to his country than he was deported to Siberia.
He came back to his native city only to suffer five years of
backbreaking work, accompanied by cold, hunger, misunderstanding and persecution of all kinds. Later he was arrested
and ill treated in prisons and camps, and he finally died of
exhaustion at the age of fifty-six. If at any of these periods
of his life he had shown any intention of giving in, his sufferings would have immediately been alleviated. Nevertheless
throughout his long Calvary one can never see the slightest
sign of his weakening. No unprejudiced observer can fail to
acknowledge Father Feodorov's loyalty and courage and admit
their only possible source: Father Leonid's realization that
the Unity of the Christian world, in full communion with the
successor of St. Peter and under his pastoral guidance, was
truly the Will of God. He thought that the immolation of his
whole life was not too great a sacrifice to actuate that Unity.

Will he be canonized one day? Those who knew his heroic
virtues ardently desire this. He certainly had the makings of
a saint, but under present circumstances, so long as liberty of
investigation does not exist in Russia, it would doubtless be
very difficult to gather all the information that is generally
required for a canonization. The Church will decide.

But as we wait, one thing seems certain. In the future,
which we hope will not be too far distant, the day will surely

come when historians will be able to speak of the division among the Christians of the East and the West as a thing of the past, as a catastrophe that occurred in the early centuries of the history of the Church as the result of the division of the Roman Empire which cradled Christianity. The same historians will not fail to commemorate with gratitude the name of Exarch Leonid Feodorov among those giants whose breadth of view and generosity of spirit raised them above the human intrigues of their time to dedicate themselves to work with all their strength to reestablish unity in the Christian world.

NOTES

Most of the information given in this biography is taken from about 300 letters and jottings written by Exarch Leonid Feodorov and other personalities mentioned in the next. About 170 of these documents were in the archives of Metropolitan Andrew Sheptitzky which are no longer available; the information was taken from accurate copies made by Prince Peter Mikholovich Volkonsky.

INTRODUCTION

1. See M. J. Rouët de Journel, S.J., *Une Russe catholique—La vie de Madame Swetchine, 1782–1857* (Paris, 1953); Comte de Falloux, *Madame Swetchine—Sa vie et ses oeuvres,* 2 vols. (Paris, 1861).

2. See C. H. Clair, S.J., "Le Prince Jean Gagarine," in *Revue du Monde Catholique,* 15 juin 1883.

3. See Peter H. Lemcke, *Life and Work of Prince Demetrius Augustine Gallitzin* (New York, Longmans Green, 1940); Daniel Sargent, *Mitri—or the Story of Prince Demetrius Augustine Gallitzin* (New York, Longmans Green, 1945).

4. For Mother Galitzine, see Louise Callan, *Philippine Duchesne* (Westminster, Md., Newman Press, 1957).

5. See Е. А. Извольская, Американские Святые и Подвижники. Русский Центр Фордамского Университета, Нью Йорк 1959.

6. О Церкви, (Berlin, B. Behr's Verlag, 1888). Церковное Предание и Русская богословская Литература по поводу критики на книгу «О Церкви.» (Fribourg, Herder, 1898).

CHAPTER ONE

1. Short autobiography which Father Feodorov wrote at the request of Metropolitan Sheptitzky in 1910 or 1911.

2. God destined Father Constantine Smirnov for a particularly productive pastoral career. After teaching religion in the upper classes of the Gymnasium, he became rector of the principal church of Kronstadt and afterward was sent on a special mission to the borders of Armenia and Persia to encourage a group of former Nestorians there who had been reunited to the Russian Orthodox Church. He was appointed auxiliary bishop of St. Petersburg and later incumbent at Tambov. In 1917 he became Metropolitan of Kazan. Patriarch Tikhon named him as one of his possible successors. He was arrested by the Bolsheviks and deported to Siberia where he succumbed to ill treatment.

CHAPTER TWO

1. Many studies on Vladimir Soloviov have been published in recent years. We have deliberately left aside the obscure question of whether or not Vladimir Soloviov died a Catholic. The reader could consult M. N. Gavrilov in *Nouvelle Revue Thélogique*, 1954, vol. 76, pp. 155–75.

2. Autobiography. See Chap. One, note 1.

3. See Yves Congar, O.P., *After Nine Hundred Years* (New York, Fordham University Press, 1959). Yves Congar, O.P., *"Divided Christendom"* (London, Centenary Press, 1904), for a deep analysis of the origin and nature of the schism.

4. See the *Russian Encyclopedia* of Brokhaus and Efrom in 41 vols. (1904), vol. 25, p. 528, under "Attacks on Religion" (Posiagatelstvo).

CHAPTER THREE

1. Metropolitan Andrew Sheptitzky died November 1, 1944. During the 43 years he remained in the Metropolitan see of Lvov, his archeparchy (or archdiocese) found itself successively under the rule of eight different political masters: Austria, Russia, again Austria, then for a short period an independent Ukrainian government, then Poland, the Soviets, the Germans and again the Soviets. Only those who are unable to disassociate religion from politics do not realize the difficulty of his position and do not understand his outstanding apostolic spirit, his sense of duty to the poor but very generous fold committed to him and also his desire to transcend human contingencies to work for Christian unity.

2. From Constantinople that school was transferred to Namur in Belgium, then to Paris. In 1946, after World War II, this institution was set up at Meudon, between Paris and Versailles, where it continues its schooling of young people of Russian origin.

3. Autobiography. See Chap. One, note 1.

4. Motu proprio, *"Dei Providentis."*

5. Autobiography. See Chap. One, note 1.

CHAPTER FOUR

1. Letter of Madame Feodorov to her son, December 1905.

2. *Ibid.*, June 1905.

3. П. М. Волконский, Краткий очерк организации Русской Католической Церкви в России. (Lvov, 1930).

4. Peter M. Volkonsky, p. 33. See note 3, this chapter.

5. Letter to Metropolitan Andrew, June 21, 1907.

6. Quoted in a letter to Metropolitan Andrew of June 10, 1906.

CHAPTER FIVE

1. A detailed account in Ukrainian and in English of these events can be found in Reverend Isidore Sochocky's *The Ukrainian Catholic Church of the Byzantine-Slavonic Rite in the U.S.A.* (Archbishop's Chancery, 815 North Franklin Street, Philadelphia 23, Pa., 1959).

2. Letter to Metropolitan Andrew, November 4, 1907.

3. *Ibid.*

4. Letter of Madame Feodorov to her son, November 18, 1905.

CHAPTER SIX

1. See Peter Volkonsky, *op. cit.*, p. 35.

2. Letter of Miss N. S. Ushakov of August 21, 1909.

3. Letter to Metropolitan Andrew of June 30, 1909.

4. Acta II, Conventus Velehradensis (Prague, 1910), p. 16.
5. Letter of Madame Feodorov to her son, September 5, 1908.
6. Letter of Metropolitan Andrew to Mgr. Isaias Papadopoulos, written in Rome February 2, 1921.
7. Letter to Metropolitan Andrew of 1910 (exact date unknown).

CHAPTER SEVEN

1. Acta I, Congressus Velehradensis (Prague, 1908), I, p. 1.
2. See Letter to Metropolitan Andrew, April 1912.
3. Testimony regarding the Exarch given by the Studite monk Nicon in 1935.
4. Letter to Metropolitan Andrew, June 11, 1912.
5. Ibid.
6. Ibid.
7. Testimony of the Studite monk Miron in 1935.
8. Letter to Metropolitan Andrew of May 7, 1913.
9. Ibid.

CHAPTER EIGHT

1. The words of this dialogue are taken from a letter of Miss Ushakov to Princess Marie Volkonsky of January 3, 1912.
2. Decree of May 22, 1908, quoted in a letter of Father Deibner to Metropolitan Andrew, January 10, 1914.
3. Letter of Miss Ushakov to Princess Marie Volkonsky, September 30, 1912.
4. Letter of Miss Ushakov to Princess Volkonsky, November 28, 1912.
5. Letter of Miss Ushakov of February 15, 1913 and of Father Deibner to Metropolitan Andrew (undated). See also Echos d'Orient, 1913, p. 26.
6. Letter of Miss Ushakov of April 8, 1913.
7. Report of Father Feodorov to Metropolitan Andrew, spring of 1914.

CHAPTER TEN

1. Letter of Metropolitan Andrew to Pope Benedict XV, August 17, 1917.
2. Letter of Mrs. C. A. Likharev to the author.

3. According to Prince Peter M. Volkonsky.

4. See Nicholas Bock's memoirs, *Russia and the Vatican on the Eve of the Revolution* (New York, Fordham University, Russian Center, 1961), p. 33.

5. Brief, *"Ex Amplissimo"* of March 1, 1921.

6. From a report of Prince Peter M. Volkonsky to the author.

7. See the Acts of the Sobor which have been published.

8. The quotation is taken from a report of Prince Peter M. Volkonsky. We did not find it in the Acts of the Sobor.

CHAPTER ELEVEN

1. Letter to Metropolitan Andrew, May 11, 1918.

2. Letter to Boris Kropp, August 19, 1918.

3. To the same, in a letter of March or April, 1920.

4. *Ibid.*

5. Letter to Metropolitan Andrew of April 1922.

6. Report to Pope Pius XI of May 5, 1922.

7. *Ibid.*

8. *Ibid.*

9. *Ibid.*

10. Letter to Metropolitan Andrew, February 1921.

11. Memoirs of Miss Julie Danzas.

12. *Ibid.*

13. *Ibid.*

14. Donald A. Lowrie, *Rebellious Prophet—A Life of Nicolai Berdyaev* (New York, Harper Brothers, 1960), p. 138 ff.

15. See *Memoirs* of Father Dimitri Kuzmine-Karavaiev.

16. See Louis J. Gallagher, S.J., *Edmund A. Walsh, S.J., A Biography* (New York, Benziger Bros., 1962).

17. Letter of Mother C. Abrikosov to Princess Marie Volkonsky, April 28, 1922.

18. Letter of Mother Abrikosov (undated).

19. Letter of Father Leonid Feodorov to Father Vladimir Abrikosov, October 30, 1922.

20. To Metropolitan Andrew, March 7, 1923.

CHAPTER TWELVE

1. Report to Pope Pius XI of May 5, 1922
2. *Ibid.*
3. *Ibid.*
4. Report of Father Potapii to Metropolitan Andrew, July 26, 1924.
5. Letter to Pope Pius XI of July 30, 1922.
6. *Ibid.*
7. Letter to Metropolitan Andrew of June 27, 1922, and also letters to Father Abrikosov of October 30 and December 13, 1922 and June 8, 1923.
8. Letter to Metropolitan Andrew, July 18, 1921.
9. Letter of May 5, 1922 to Pope Pius XI and of December 10, 1922, to the Very Reverend Vladimir Ledochowski, S.J.

CHAPTER THIRTEEN

1. Letter to Metropolitan Andrew of March or April 1921.
2. Letter to Metropolitan Andrew, April 21, 1921.
3. Letter to Metropolitan Andrew, July 18, 1921.
4. Report of May 5, 1922 to Pope Pius XI.
5. *Ibid.*
6. Letter to Metropolitan Andrew, August 1, 1921.
7. From a report of Father Vladimir Abrikosov.
8. Letter to Metropolitan Andrew, April 1921.
9. Letter to Father Abrikosov, December 13, 1922.
10. *Ibid.*
11. Letter to the Very Reverend Vladimir Ledochowski, S. J.

CHAPTER FOURTEEN

1. Memoirs of Miss Danzas.
2. *Ibid.*

3. *Ibid.*

4. The Moscow trial was reported at length in several publications: *New York Herald* of April 6, 1923; News Service of the NCWC, May 21, 1923; *La Civiltà Cattolica*, July 1923, p. 152 ff.; *The Bolshevik Persecution of Christianity* by Captain Francis McCullagh (London, John Murray, 1924).

CHAPTER FIFTEEN

1. See note 4, Chap. 14.
2. Letter to Metropolitan Andrew, July 1, 1923.
3. Memoirs of Miss Danzas.
4. See note 2, this chapter.
5. Letter to Father Edmund Walsh of May 8, 1923.
6. Letter to Metropolitan Andrew of April 25, 1923.
7. Letter to Father Edmund Walsh, July 22, 1923 and May 27, 1923.
8. Letter to Very Reverend Vladimir Ledochowski, S.J., May 27, 1923.
9. To Father V. Abrikosov, June 8, 1923.
10. Letter to Metropolitan Andrew of July 1, 1923.

CHAPTER SIXTEEN

1. Letter to a friend of Metropolitan Andrew who was to hand the content to the Metropolitan, May 23, 1926.

CHAPTER SEVENTEEN

1. Boris Solonevitch, *Dans la tempête bolchevique* (Paris, Spes, 1939).
2. Memoirs of Miss Danzas. The other details are taken from reports of other prisoners who are still on the other side of the Iron Curtain. It seems wiser not to publish their names.

CHAPTER EIGHTEEN

1. This incident is related in the preface written by Bishop Sloskan to a short biography in Italian of the Exarch by Vittorio Lodi (Rome, Traveri Editore).

2. Memoirs of a prisoner. See Chap. 19, note 2.

3. Memoirs of Miss Danzas.

CHAPTER NINETEEN

1. Letter of Father Ilguin to the author, August 25, 1935.

Index

INDEX

DATE DUE